Praise for
INVESTMENTS UNLIMITED

"This book does an amazing job of explaining how good DevOps practices can help ensure that your software is safe, secure, and auditable. I learned a lot from it, which I can't say often after reading DevOps books over the last ten years. This is a must read for any CISO or executive looking to improve the security and compliance practices in their organization."

—**Ross Clanton**, Chief Architect and Managing Director,
American Airlines

"*Investments Unlimited* builds upon years of DevSecOps literature while firmly anchoring the principles into regulated entities like financial services. The technology fable will keep you engaged with relatable stories, conversations, and practical knowledge for you to implement at your own firm and inside your team."

—**Dr. Branden R. Williams**, VP IAM Strategy, Ping Identity

"Finally we have a book that can be leveraged by everyone in your organization involved in meeting security, audit, and compliance requirements. You'll be able to apply this practical guidance immediately, and I really appreciate the inclusion of all of the functions and roles required to be successful. It's a great reminder that we are all in this together!"

—**Courtney Kissler**, CTO, Zulily

"Today, software developers are just as much security engineers, whether they know it or not. In a unique and compelling way, *Investments Unlimited* illustrates how to safely automate security testing, audit, and compliance to help organizations move faster and safer. It's a fast and fun story that sheds light on a much needed subject: the importance of bringing security, audit, and compliance out of the shadows and into the everyday life of a developer. Security, audit, and compliance are everyone's job every day. *Investments Unlimited* joyfully brings to light that these essential functions are enabled by DevOps."

—**Jim Manico**, Founder and Secure Coding Educator,
Manicode Security

T0283822

A Novel about DevOps, Security, Audit Compliance, and Thriving in the Digital Age

INVESTMENTS UNLIMITED

By

Helen Beal	Michael Edenzon	John Rzeszotarski
Bill Bensing	Tapabrata Pal	Andres Vega
Jason Cox	Caleb Queern	John Willis

IT Revolution
Portland, Oregon

25 NW 23rd Pl, Suite 6314
Portland, OR 97210

First Edition
Printed in the United States of America

27 26 25 24 23 22   2 3 4 5 6 7 8 9 10

Cover and book design by Devon Smith

Library of Congress Control Number: 2022935846

ISBN: 9781950508532
eBook ISBN: 9781950508549
Web PDF ISBN: 9781950508563

For information about special discounts for bulk purchases or for information on booking authors for an event, please visit our website at www.ITRevolution.com.

INVESTMENTS UNLIMITED

To all those change agents in every organization
who dare to challenge the status quo,
build bridges instead of walls,
and propel us into the unlimited future.

CONTENTS

Investments Unlimited Directory   ix
Preface   xi
Prelude   xiii

Chapter 1   1
Chapter 2   9
Chapter 3   19
Chapter 4   27
Chapter 5   33
Chapter 6   45
Chapter 7   53
Chapter 8   61
Chapter 9   73
Chapter 10   83
Chapter 11   91
Chapter 12   105
Chapter 13   117
Epilogue   127

Appendix 1: MRAs and MRIAs   129
Appendix 2: Pipeline Design with Control Tollgates   131
Appendix 3: DevSecOps Manifesto   133
Appendix 4: Shift Left   134
Appendix 5: Software Composition Analysis   136
Appendix 6: US Executive Order on Improving the Nation's Cybersecurity   137
Appendix 7: FAQ   138

Acknowledgments   141
About the Authors   145

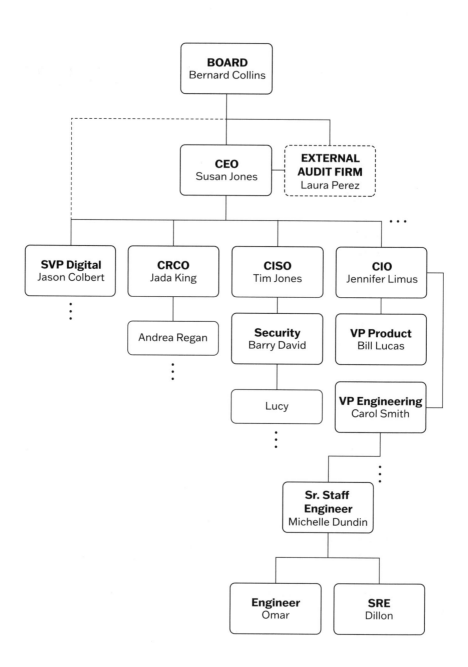

INVESTMENTS UNLIMITED DIRECTORY

Bernard Collins, Chairman of the Board
Susan Jones, CEO

Jason Colbert, SVP Digital Transformation
Jada King, Chief Risk and Compliance Officer (CRCO)
Tim Jones, Chief Information Security Officer (CISO)
Jennifer Limus, SVP of Engineering and Chief Information Officer (CIO)
Bill Lucas, VP of Product
Carol Smith, VP of Engineering, Digital Banking

Michelle Dundin, Senior Staff Engineer
Barry David, Security
Andrea Regan, Audit & Risk
Omar, Staff Engineer
Dillon, Staff Site Reliability Engineer
Lucy, Security

Laura Perez, External Audit Firm

PREFACE

Governance. People have multiple reactions to that word. To some, it brings about anxiety, frustration, fear, and anger. To others, it means control, the maintenance of peace, order, and safety. Whatever reaction you may have to that word, you'll likely find that you are somehow responsible for either maintaining or complying with governance to some degree.

IT governance in the enterprise is hard. Regardless of the reaction you have to the concept itself, there is a great deal of difficulty in doing governance well. Like any process, governance seeks to provide controls to safeguard the treasures that a company holds of value, which include people, data, brands, and products. Sadly, the execution of governance in practice often creates massive friction, frustration, and failure for the teams attempting to deliver value for their organizations.

This book tells the story of Investments Unlimited, Inc. (IUI), a fictional company in the financial sector. But the same tale can be told about any industry or enterprise that deals with governance.

The goal of this book is to help enterprises radically rethink governance and how software is built inside the enterprise. By introducing concepts, tools, and ideas to reimagine governance, we seek to catalyze a more humane way to enable high-velocity software delivery that inspires trust and is inherently more secure.

As you travel through this narrative, we hope you pick up modern ways to view, deploy, use, and survive governance in a fun way that helps deliver organizational objectives. Ultimately, what you take away will make it easier for you to deliver business value better, faster, safer, and happier.

—The Authors

PRELUDE

"Dad? Bad news."

The rain against the government office window on the gray New England afternoon had gotten so strong that Greg Dorshaw had to ask his teenage daughter to repeat herself. His old flip phone was getting harder to hear.

"Dad, they called off the game because of the weather. You don't need to come. Drive safely on your way home."

Dorshaw never missed his daughter's softball games. This week, the wet Boston weather had given the Supervisory Officer an excuse to stay late in the office and dig into a curious email he had received from his team earlier that day.

Eager for some quiet time to focus, he turned off the fluorescent lights in his Federal Reserve Board office, poked at what remained of his takeout Pad Thai, and focused on the email. With his face lit only by the light of the monitor, he read:

Subject Line: IUI preliminary examination results

Greg, looks like history is repeating itself. Seems like another fintech firm is going to require a formal action.

The team is quite concerned . . .

CHAPTER 1

Monday, March 28th

Susan Jones had been the CEO of Investments Unlimited, Inc. (IUI), for five years. She was quick on her feet and always appeared to ask the right questions and make the right decisions. The board trusted her. But right now—although you couldn't tell from her demeanor—she was panicking.

"How did you find out?" Susan said into the phone, nearly gasping. It was family pizza night, but she had stepped away from the kitchen to take the urgent call. Behind her the noise of her family, Rich and Lucas making Rich's famous pizza, seemed to disappear. All she could hear was the beat of her own heart and Jason, her SVP of Digital Transformation, on the phone.

"I met with Bernard this evening at our regular two-finger Scotch session. He let me know that the MRIA[1] will be issued to IUI." Jason paused. "You know, it may feel like regulators are out to get us, but they're really there to help us and help protect our customers."

"You could have fooled me," Susan replied, half under her breath. She didn't think Jason heard her as he kept talking.

"It's not uncommon for an MRIA to be informally notified through back channels so there's no surprise when it's issued. Bernard has a good relationship with the director of the regulatory agency approving the MRIA. That director reached out to Bernard as a show of good faith," Jason said.

Susan took a deep breath. She was familiar with an MRIA, a Matter Requiring Immediate Attention, but only in concept. Actually being issued one was alarming. Federal regulators only issue an MRIA when something is seriously wrong at a bank. They aren't handed out like candy. Susan had heard horror stories from other institutions, but she'd never had one issued at a bank she worked at—let alone the bank she ran.

"Do you know what the MRIA is about?" Susan asked.

---

1. For more details on MRAs (Matters Requiring Attention) and MRIAs (Matters Requiring Immediate Attention), please refer to Appendix 1.

"Yes, and it's frankly embarrassing. There are over fifteen MRAs that have been issued to IUI over the past year. We've asked for several extensions on those, but there doesn't seem to be a clear plan to close them. That's why this MRIA is being issued. Our team hasn't provided any evidence of progress, and the agency now thinks we have a huge problem."

"I see," Susan said. But really, she didn't understand at all. *How did my team let this happen?* she wondered. *How did I let this happen?* Her CAO (Chief Audit Officer) had repeatedly assured her that everything was in order with these MRAs. Clearly that wasn't true.

"As you know, it's a big issue," Jason said. "Just remember, you're CEO because Bernard thinks the world of you and knows you're extremely capable. I reminded him that he couldn't have retired without you. He agreed."

"Thanks for the kind words, Jason. We'll have to get the whole team together first thing in the morning to tackle how we found ourselves in such a mess. There's nothing more we can do tonight."

"Sounds good," responded Jason. "I'm sorry to interrupt your evening, but I knew you would want to know. I'll talk to you tomorrow. Have a good night."

"Yes, thanks, Jason. I'm glad you called. Good night." Susan ended the call and sat down at the dining room table. It was a long table that fit over fifteen people, and it was always made up as if there was a dinner party starting at any moment. The orderly array of dishes in front of her seemed to mock her as she processed the implications of the call with Jason. Her mind was racing for answers and solutions.

She sat there, waiting for the numbness to wear off, waiting for her thoughts to slow down to a crawl.

"Love, are you okay?" Rich asked softly as he walked out of the kitchen.

"Yes, I'm fine. Give me a minute, and I'll come in to help with the pizza," Susan replied. She could smell the old Sicilian tomato sauce recipe that Rich was cooking up. It was a favorite of his, handed down from his great-grandmother to his mother to him. She took a deep breath. The delicious aroma was like therapy. Maybe she was starting to feel better—or maybe she was just hungry. Either way, she walked into the kitchen.

As Susan looked around, all she could see was a mess. White flour covered the countertops and floors. It looked like a fresh coat of Aspen snow had covered their kitchen.

"Well, this is certainly a 'matter requiring immediate attention' if I've ever seen one," Susan said, walking over to her six-year-old son, Lucas, happily drawing smiley faces in the flour on the countertop.

"No need to meet Jason this evening?" Rich asked, bringing Susan an apron.

"Nope, the phone call did enough damage for one night," Susan responded, tying the apron on.

"Ohhhhh, did Mommy get in trouuuble?" Lucas asked as he wiped his flour-covered hands all over Susan's once-clean apron.

"Oh, Lucas," Rich reprimanded gently. "Mommy didn't get in trouble. There's just a problem at her work. But she'll fix it. That's why she's the boss," Rich said with a smile toward his wife. He placed a big round of pizza dough on the counter in front of them. Flour flew up into the air, and Lucas laughed.

"What kind of problem?" Lucas asked as Susan spread sauce over the dough. "Did you talk while your boss was talking? Or break a rule? 'Cause Xian broke a rule at recess today, and he had to sit for the rest of recess and not play at all."

"No, I didn't break a rule," Susan said. "There's just some housecleaning at work that hasn't been getting done like it should. And now we have a whole lot of cleaning to do in a short amount of time."

"Is it like when Grandma comes for a visit and you get all crazy?" Lucas asked, dramatically flinging his arms around.

Rich stifled a laugh and turned to grab the toppings.

"No, no. It's more like when I ask you to clean your room. That's like an MRA—what we call a Matter Requiring Attention," Susan said, adopting her most serious movie-trailer voice.

"I hate when you tell me to clean my room."

"Yes, well, what's happened is we've been asked to clean our room lots of times, but apparently no one has done it, or at least not very well, so now we have to deal with a MR-*I*-A, a Matter Requiring *Immediate* Attention."

Lucas's eyes widened.

"Think of it like you're on your last warning and you're about to get a time out," Rich added. "Or get sent to the principal's office."

"Wow. Mommy really *did* get in trouble," Lucas said. Then he reached for a huge handful of mozzarella and dropped it in the center of the pizza.

Susan suddenly realized she needed to inform her leadership team and set aside time tomorrow for assessing the situation.

"Rich, give me about five minutes before we top the pizzas. I need to do one last thing."

Susan hurried back into the dining room and fired off a quick message to her senior staff using the inter-office chat system.

"*Sorry to break into your evening, everyone, but this news can't wait. Jason and I were informed of an MRIA coming our way. Please do what you can to clear your schedules between 10 and 2 tomorrow. We have a lot of work to do.*"

She pressed send and walked back into the kitchen.

Susan settled into her side of the bed as Rich pulled up the latest episode of the comfort TV show they were watching these days.

"So, you've got quite a firestorm to settle at the office, huh?" Rich asked.

"Yes. An MRIA is no joke," Susan explained.

"If I recall correctly, isn't the next step some type of formal action by the regulators?" asked Rich.

"Yes, it is. Something like that would have a devastating impact on IUI and everyone who works there. No doubt it could end Bernard's time as chairman, finish my career, and tarnish me for the rest of my working life. If it gets to that point, there are many companies looking to purchase our assets in a fire sale." Susan frowned as she said all of this.

"You'll figure it out. They didn't make you CEO for nothing." Rich clicked the button on the remote and started the show.

Susan's mind wandered. She reflected back on how IUI had started fifteen years ago as a small company in a crowded industry clamoring for business. Like those nearby research centers, they sought to discover new ways to deliver investment and banking value to the world. She remembered the lean years where they struggled to get by.

In just the past twelve years, this small but big-hearted company had managed to not only survive but also thrive with its winning strategy of focusing on socially responsible investing. This differentiator resonated in the market and soon began to pay off. Three years later, the one hundred–person firm had expanded to a thousand employees and just topped $400 million in revenue and total assets of $20 billion. Things were looking pretty good.

They had also recently begun a digital transformation utilizing the business-accelerating principles of Agile and DevOps. Jason had been hired to help with this. He was given the charter to take intuitive digital products to the next level. He had a bold vision. He wanted to completely redesign the user experience, making complex financial transactions and products approachable, easy, safe, and reliable. He was doing all of this while helping their teams adopt more modern and Agile ways of working. The first releases of these intuitive tools or digital products proved to be way better than expected. Feedback from customers was astounding and conversion rates for new accounts were growing faster than ever. It felt like the next voyage of IUI was just about to set sail!

But now things were looking a little more like a sinking ship.

Susan wasn't sure how she had found herself in such an uncomfortable position. She had assembled a great team to lead IUI into the future. Her CIO, Jennifer Limus, was brilliant. As a developer turned leader, Jennifer always seemed to have her finger on the pulse of technological innovation.

How did this get so out of hand? Susan thought to herself.

Susan wondered if she would be able to sleep. Her mind was spinning, searching for answers. Eventually she was able to drift off, dreaming of ships sinking under her kitchen faucets, dinner plates bobbing in the water, and regulators shouting from the countertops.

Tuesday, March 29th

Susan arrived in the company board room ahead of everyone else. Her admin accompanied her to set up the virtual teleconference, place the printed MRIA documents on the table, and adjust the lighting. Susan took her seat and looked out the window. Clouds were gathering. *An apt metaphor*, she thought to herself.

Jennifer, the CIO; Tim, the CISO; Bill, VP of Product; and Jada, the Chief Risk and Compliance Officer (CRCO),[2] arrived a few minutes later and took their seats around the table. It was clear that everyone was anxious and tensions were high.

"Well, you all know why we're here today," Susan began. "I need answers, and fast. But first, I'd like to announce to everyone that effective today, Jada will act as Chief Risk and Compliance Officer, heading both Audit as well as Risk."

Murmurings began to fly around the room. Susan quickly held her hand up, a clear sign for everyone to quiet down. "I want to make this clear. No one has been fired. Fredrick has been looking to retire, and he has taken this as an opportunity to finally spend more time at that cabin of his and teach his grandkids to fish. I wish him the very best. I'll be looking to fill the void he left, but it will take a while. I have every confidence in Jada's abilities until then."

Even with Susan's attempts to quell the fear in the room, it was clear that everyone was tense. She understood. It had been a hard discussion with Fredrick early this morning. Despite her best attempts to assure Fredrick that she didn't pass blame to him, he had made it clear that he didn't feel he was up to the task anymore and that he had full confidence in Jada taking over.

"Okay, everyone. Now that that is out of the way, let's get down to business. I've heard what Fredrick had to say, but now I want to hear from all of you. How did we get to the point where the OCC has hit us with an MRIA?"

Immediately, Jada spoke up. Jada had been with IUI as long as Susan, and she was always quick to offer her opinions. Her passion had made her a great CRO, and

----

2   One of the themes that continues to evolve is the interaction and relationship between the chief audit executive (CAE) and the chief risk officer (CRO). The roles of these positions are highly interrelated and interdependent. In fact, in many organizations they are merged into a single role, such as CRCO.

hopefully a great CRCO. But that same strength also made her come across as rigid and abrasive at times.

"I've been warning everyone about this for the past year," Jada answered, looking around the room. She added, "Yet consistently I was told that product release deadlines were a higher priority."

"Come on, Jada. You know we had no choice," Bill said. As VP of Product, Bill was obsessed with shipping features and products that would delight clients and drive revenue. He was always pushing to get things done and could always be counted on to defend his team. He had been with IUI longer than anyone else in the room and knew their customer well. He was sometimes slower to accept new mindsets and ways of working, but his intentions were right. "Without these new features and updates, the apps would be deemed unusable, and our customers would vote us off the island. It's like the Risk team doesn't even know we're running a competitive business here."

"Of course we know that, Bill. We're trying to help protect IUI and its competitiveness," Jada responded. "We can't be competitive if our applications and customer data aren't secure. I've been cautioning you guys that we've let our delivery teams do whatever they want in the name of DevOps and digital transformation. We have no control. For heaven's sake, we are a bank!"

Susan leaned back in her chair. She wasn't pleased by the blame that was being tossed around the room.

"Jada's right," Tim began in his typical firm yet calm voice, obviously trying to rein in a discussion that was quickly taking a bad turn. "We're all looking out for IUI."

Tim had a commanding and official presence about him that fit his role as CISO. When he entered the room, people paid attention. His résumé included a long list of leading financial cyber groups, as well as some large IT audit firms. "To be fair," he continued, "we have all of these MRAs listed in the product backlog. Why hasn't the Dev team been delivering on them?"

Bill rolled his eyes. "Honestly, it seems to take forever to just get features out. I don't know what our Dev teams do all day. They clearly can't keep up."

"Keep up?!" Jennifer looked perplexed. She was probably one of the youngest executive leaders at a company the size of IUI, but her knowledge and skill far outweighed many of her peers at other institutions. "I think everyone understands that we attack whatever is in our multiple backlogs with the engineers we have available. But each product's backlog is growing on a daily basis with new features and demands." Jennifer looked over at Bill and continued, "The problem is we never get enough time to address technical debt, much less the frequent 'urgent new feature' fire drills that the Product team keeps hitting us with."

"So hire more people!" Bill shot back.

"You think it's that easy? It's not. The demand for quality engineers is extremely competitive, and then we still have to onboard those we do hire. We have many open spots right now, and the new engineers we just hired are still coming up to speed. I don't think any of us saw the tsunami of new feature work that would be hitting us." Jennifer took a deep breath, obviously trying, then looked over at Susan for support.

Susan sat at the head of the table, quietly watching and listening as her team bickered like teenagers. She had expected some finger-pointing, but this was worse than she imagined. Most of all, she was just confused. She had been receiving enthusiastic reports from all of her VPs about the great progress they had made with DevOps over the past few years. And after IUI had brought Jason in a year ago as SVP of Digital Transformation, the progress had only increased. However, now it seemed like the left hand didn't know what the right had been doing.

"Look, this isn't productive," Susan said, standing up. "I need some real answers. What is the current situation with the MRAs and what are we going to do about it? I need to show the board that we have a clear plan of action. The regulators have informed us that we have just three months to address all of their concerns and show we have a plan to move forward. Three months before IUI gets hit with a formal enforcement action from the regulators. Three months before every one of you and every person who works for you is suddenly out of job or IUI is taken over by the government.[3] Three months before everything we have built comes crashing down around us.

"Now, I don't think anyone in this room wants to have to tell their entire team that their leaders failed them." Susan paused and looked at each person around the table. She was relieved to see some of them squirm slightly under her gaze. It meant the message was hitting home.

"We get it," Jada said, breaking the silence. She took a breath. "The MRAs that led to this MRIA deal with a lot of issues related to our IT governance—the way we develop, run, and manage our software. We'll get a summary list for you."

"Thank you," Susan said, sitting back down in her chair and looking at Tim, who was sitting next to Jada.

Tim looked at Jennifer, then back to Susan. "I'll work with Jennifer to put together our action plan to get these addressed. But it isn't going to be easy. We have a lot of work going on right now . . . "

"There's always a lot of work going on," Susan interrupted. "And I don't need to be told that this will be hard. What I need are solutions. IUI's survival could be in jeopardy, with serious consequences to our thousands of employees and their families. This must be our top priority."

---

3 You can view a real cease and desist order issued against MUFG Bank here: https://www.occ.gov/news-issuances/news-releases/2021/nr-occ-2021-100.html.

Susan looked around the room and worked up a grim smile. "I know we can get through this. There's plenty of talent in this room and on your teams. We have just three months to fix this mess or it's game over. It's as simple as that."

Susan stood again. "Now, I have to go and meet with the board, who will likely want us to bring in an external auditor to review and sign off on our closure package with regulators. But I want regular updates on your progress. My assistant will be putting a weekly huddle on all of your calendars. I expect great things from you all. Let's figure this out. Let's make this happen."

Heads nodded. Susan grabbed her tablet and exited the room.

CHAPTER 2

Tuesday, March 29th (*continued*)

"Okay everyone, let's do this!" Tim announced. He was standing at the front of a conference room crammed with VPs and SVPs. He had been in meetings like this many times before. Everyone was here to defend their territory, to just say they were part of it, or to sit back, listen, and then complain later.

Tim looked around the room. Carol, the VP of Engineering Digital Banking, was seated right across from him, and Bill was seated across from Jada. Each of the political nemeses were now face to face without Susan refereeing.

Let the melee begin, he thought, was tamping down his feigned enthusiasm.

"Carol, let's get you up to speed," Tim began. "Jada, Bill, Jennifer, and I met with Susan earlier today regarding the MRIA we received. Has Jennifer filled you in on the conversation?"

"Yes, yes, Jennifer and I met earlier, and she gave me the rundown. If I understand it correctly, we shot ourselves in the foot by not responding adequately to these MRAs over the past twelve months. I think it was something like fifteen MRAs that either we didn't respond to or our response was sub par?" Carol shared.

"That's right," Tim responded. "Today's agenda is simple. We must compile a list of the findings. We will then review this list with Susan and our progress on addressing the actions in the weekly huddles with her and, likely, an external audit team, until we submit our response to the regulators in three months."

Bill quickly interrupted. "What do we do about the big release? Our teams have been working on Project Prisma for the last few quarters. We can't cancel that."

"Really? What do we do when we're shut down?" Jada shot back.

"Obviously we need to keep the business running while addressing the MRIA," Tim jumped in, hoping to quell yet another fight between Product and Risk.

"Let's take a step back. What kept us from addressing these issues right up front? Why haven't we responded to the MRAs sufficiently? What's the bottleneck?"

Bill furrowed his brow. "Are we talking about the MRIA or the MRAs? I'm totally confused now."

"If we had responded to the MRAs in time and adequately, we wouldn't have the MRIA." Tim sounded a little exasperated.

"Well, we did push back on several of these MRA findings," Carol spoke up. "We asked questions on the ones that don't make sense or don't apply. But we got radio silence. Zero response!" She turned to Jada. "We get no help from the Risk or Audit teams."

Jada looked puzzled.

Carol looked back at Tim. "See?! That's the problem. We not only have to manage our engineering projects but we have to shepherd all this paperwork to get stuff done here. I don't have enough people to do that. And it sure isn't in our backlogs."

"Yes, yes, I get it!" snapped Tim. "I understand the bickering, but that isn't helping right now. We are here today to identify the issues raised in MRAs that led to this MRIA and then report back to Susan." Tim felt like a broken record.

Carol sighed. "It always falls to Engineering to fix everything. I won't have all the blame game going against my developers. Engineering is about building things, building bridges across seemingly impossible problems and arriving at new destinations. I know some people here have little appreciation for the role, but there are great rewards in seeing good outcomes.

"I'm inviting Michelle, one of my senior staff engineers, to this meeting," Carol announced. "She has historically raised compliance concerns, and she'll be an asset to this conversation." Carol turned to her phone and typed a message on the interoffice chat system.

"It's terrifying that Engineering and Product have no clue how to manage risk," Jada said, warming up her artillery.

"Isn't that your job?" Bill responded with a smug smile.

"Ugh." Tim sat down. It looked as though he had given up on refereeing the meeting. The conversation went on like this for several more minutes, a constant stream of back and forth, not one of the prize-fighters addressing the single action for the meeting that Tim had laid out.

"Okay, we aren't getting anywhere," Tim said loudly, raising his arms to quell the discussion that had risen several octaves in the last five minutes alone. "So much complaining," he stated, as if he epitomized a glass house. "You all are starting to sound like my kids fighting each other when I tell them to clean their room. I'm always amazed at the big mess they create while trying to clean up the small mess. Truth is, it's simply because they spite each other rather than work together."

Michelle arrived like a whirlwind and the room went silent. Her arms were full of a laptop, tablet, paper notebook, and pen. She sat down next to Carol and hastily arranged her stuff on the table. Her long black hair was pulled back into a ponytail and her eyes were bright. She looked poised for action and clearly had something to say.

Carol introduced her to the room, most of whom had never met or worked with her directly. "Michelle is one of my best engineers, despite the fact that she's been at IUI the shortest of anyone else in this room. But there's no doubt in my mind that she needs to be here. Since Michelle joined IUI from a smaller company, she's brought with her a youthful energy and knowledge of the latest ways of working. She doesn't shrink from expressing her opinions, even to senior leadership." Carol looked pointedly around the room. "She's a change agent. And that's exactly why Jason had recommended her for the job, and why we need her to help with this mess."

"But does she have the necessary experience . . ." Jada began.

"After she joined IUI as a junior engineer, Michelle soon took on the mantle of security liaison for the entire Engineering team," Carol interrupted. "She's worked with Tim's group conducting code reviews of applications all across IUI. And she's been responsible for answering questions that come up during PCI DSS[1] compliance reviews. She even coauthored the annual state of security report."

"Okay, okay," Jada said. "Sounds like she's a good person to help us out. Let's hear what she has to say."

"I knew this was going to happen," Michelle said firmly and succinctly. "I sent out a memo months ago warning everyone about this exact scenario, but everyone was too busy to pay attention? Well, here we are. I told you that our manual, one-size-fits-all security review with IUI's large portfolio of applications was a disaster waiting to happen. Our software development life cycle risk reduction practices are just too immature. And on top of that, we've been ignoring the findings from our own Audit team."

Bill snapped in response. "If Security and Audit would get us a unified set of requirements and work with us to comply without slowing us down so much, we'd be in a better place." Bill's frustration was evident in his voice and on his face. "We're constantly balancing competing requirements for the IUI portfolio. What we need to be doing is delivering value to our customers. You try doing that while juggling competing priorities from the business."

"Bill, not to be too much of a punk, but I do that. Me! It all rolls downhill, and guess who has two thumbs and is at the bottom? This person," Michelle said, her thumbs pointing at her face as she stood up for herself. Carol smirked.

A short, tense pause was felt in the room. "Audit doesn't have requirements," Jada broke in. "Audit's role is simple. We look at the controls, what IUI says it should do to manage risk, and compare it to what we actually do. Audit doesn't make the rules—heck, they don't even recommend controls. Audit answers the question: Is IUI doing what they say they should be doing?"

"That's not true. This time last year I remember getting a long list of 'thou shalts' from Audit. It's like you all intentionally keep the details to yourself and then slap our

---

1 Payment Card Industry Data Security Standard: https://www.pcisecuritystandards.org/.

hands when we don't read your minds!" Bill shot back. "If I can't get requirements from you, then where do we get them from?"

Tim quickly interrupted, "Jada, Bill . . . hold those thoughts. We're supposed to report to Susan on the MRIA. We need this exact conversation but not right now."

Michelle quickly followed up. "I suggest we break down the audit finding into stages and then try to understand what technology and process improvements need to be applied." She opened her laptop to begin reading the summary of the findings.

"Michelle, I appreciate the enthusiasm, but let's take this up a level," Tim replied. "The MRIA has summarized all the previous findings. It states here in the Executive Summary: *Inconsistent process, ineffective in ensuring security and compliance, resulting in unauthorized and vulnerable software with significant number of defects being released to production.*"

"That tells us nothing!" Michelle stated passionately. "Inconsistent process? Well, hashtag-facepalm, duh. This is only telling us what we already know." Frantically scrolling through the report on her screen, Michelle followed up with, "Where in here do they tell us specifically what we need to fix?"

"They don't and they won't," replied Jada. "That report only tells us what we already know: we aren't following our own processes, and our processes may be missing something. It's our job to respond with what we will do to address that concern. Where are the teams storing their processes these days? The Risk organization stores all its information and tracking details in our GRC system."

Just mentioning the Governance, Risk, and Compliance system caused an audible groan in the room. Jada didn't even pretend to be shocked. Her own teams even complained about the GRC system and its impossible user interface.

"Engineering teams document their processes in markdown and source control them in our Git repositories. The same area where we store code," Michelle responded.

"Security is supposed to capture info and store it in the knowledge management module of our internal service system," Tim added.

"Product tracks all of its requirements in our ticketing system," Bill said.

"Four organizations and four different places to store information. That seems like a red flag," Carol said. "Michelle, how do the engineers use each of these systems?"

"Engineering takes its marching orders from the ticketing system the Product team uses. We live our lives in that system. In general, no one in engineering knows about the GRC system. Nor do they care. I only know about it by researching compliance issues we had with a release a couple quarters ago. As for the knowledge management system, well . . ." A sudden pause filled the room, then Michelle continued. "We know about it, and most of us have access. Although we don't use it. Most of the information is incomplete, out of date, or inaccurate. If we have a security issue or question, we back channel it. If we can't back channel it, we consider it a good old college try, then move on. Our best security advice mostly comes from internet searches."

Tim barely managed to keep a straight face as he heard Michelle's last comment.

Carol said, "If you're the most in-the-know person, and this is how you operate, this looks like something we need to consider. How can we ever do what we say we are doing if we can't figure out where to go to do the things we need to do?"

"I swear I read that same sentence in a Dr. Suess book before," Bill quipped.

"Our response to Susan is becoming a bit clearer now," Tim interjected. Everyone turned their heads toward him, all with confused expressions. "We can't tell her what's wrong when we collectively don't know specifically what the issue is. All we know is, somehow, someway, the full process is broken. Bits and pieces may work in silos, but it doesn't work as a full system, and I'm broadly speaking when I use the word 'system.'"

"Then what should our response be?" Jada asked everyone around the table.

"I have an idea," Tim said, regaining control of the conversation. "Michelle has the best grasp on how things operate. She has proven she's able to work across all of our areas." He looked at Michelle. "Michelle, how long would it take you to dig deeper, read the specific MRAs, and come up with a current state and the basis of a proposal for a future state?"

Feeling a bit under the gun, Michelle responded, "Are you asking me to figure out how to respond to the MRIA?"

"No, not at all," Tim replied. "Think of it as an outline with a sole focus on listing the specific issues. We'll collectively build a response, but first, and to your point earlier, we need specifics."

"Okay, sure. What's the timeline?" Michelle asked.

"Today is Tuesday, and the weekly huddle is every Thursday," Tim said.

"Well, we won't have the details this Thursday. I don't think that any quality research can be done with what remains of today and tomorrow."

"Yes, I agree," Tim interrupted. "Let's meet next Wednesday, same time and place. That gives you a week. Remember, we aren't looking for solutions right now; we're simply looking for an outline. The best outline would be based upon, and I'll restate what Jada said earlier, *what we say we should be doing and what we are, or are not, doing.*"

All eyes were on Michelle. She sat there deep in thought. She didn't appear to be under pressure. Rather, she appeared to contemplate if the time was satisfactory for the required research. A few seconds passed as if they were ten long minutes.

"Carol, Bill, I need to offload some work to the team today. To make this happen, this needs to be my only focus. I have enough research so far that I'm confident I can have an outline by next Wednesday if I'm not also trying to do other work."

"Okay, good. Remember, while you're accountable for this, you don't have to be the only person to actually do the work. Bill, can you assist Michelle?" Tim asked.

Bill looked bewildered. His organization's backlogs were so backed up that each backlog had a backlog item to review the backlog! He had his own process issues to figure out with Marketing, Sales, and Finance. But Bill knew this was not a question but a political "volun-told" situation. He didn't have to agree. After all, he didn't report to Tim. But he knew how important this was. Bill had a keen sense that work like this may become a mainstay for him, and his organization, in the future. This was important.

Bill replied with a simple, "Yes, I can."

"Okay, so we have a plan," Tim said. "Come next Wednesday, Michelle and Bill will have a draft outline of the things we say we are doing and the reality of how we are or are not doing them. To ensure as much clarity as possible, we must keep our scope to the poorly answered MRAs addressed under the MRIA statement in the executive summary."

Tim looked around the room. Everyone nodded in agreement. A rush of optimism swept the room. It felt like things were finally starting to move.

"Tim, why don't you, Jada, and I stop by Susan's office to set expectations?" Carol said, as it was evident the meeting was coming to a close.

"Agreed," replied Tim. "This MRIA is a ticking time bomb."

Wednesday, March 30th

Michelle and Bill showed up to the office the next day at their usual time. Bill wandered over to Michelle's cube around 9:30 AM.

"Morning, Bill," Michelle said.

"Good morning to you as well. So, do you have a recommendation for where we start?"

"Yes, yes I do. I combed through all of my emails and previous research last night. I moved it all to a new folder on the shared drive called 'MRIA Madness.' More of an ode to March Madness; less about our own madness."

Bill chuckled a bit. He thought the title was witty.

"First thing I'll do today is speak again with each of the people I've talked with to generate this research. I started a document called *1 - MRIA Outline*. I added the '1' to it so it's the first document when you open the share drive."

"Good call," Bill replied.

"I'll summarize my findings in this document and link to any other relevant information. My approach is to start with Risk and Audit. I want to trace the process starting with us stating 'this is what we do.' I've decided to give a single word to these 'things we do.' I'm calling them promises. 'This is what we do' is a promise we are making to regulators and customers and to each other."

"That's actually brilliant, Michelle," Bill replied. "Putting my Product hat on, that would be a good way to market any change management we need behind this. Controls are very sterile, but promises—well, no one wants to break a promise."

Michelle smiled, recognizing the compliment. "Sure. Thanks, Bill," she said. "After I find all these promises, I'm going to trace each one to some type of implementation. We need to see how we commit to keeping these promises we make. It's basic, but it's a start. I don't want to over complicate the discovery process. What do you think of the approach?"

"Ship it," Bill replied. "How about you and I meet up at 3:00 PM every day? I'll set aside two hours to analyze your info and help compile the outline. Does that work for you?"

"Sure, works for me!"

This first day seemed to be the longest and shortest day at the same time. Michelle spent every minute hopping around the office. No one was outside her scope of calendar invites and office drop-ins. She was pleased to find that many of the people she talked to were more than willing to help.

During it all, she realized a very important aspect of humanity. People love to talk about themselves, especially when someone is listening to them moan about a problem. Even though Michelle was still fairly junior in her career, she had a natural knack for facilitating unstructured conversation.

For one meeting, Bill joined. He was impressed with how she led the conversation with empathy. She often said things like "I know what you mean. I felt the same way," or "I can see how that was difficult for you." Bill on the other hand was visibly annoyed by some of their criticisms, demeanor, and complaints. He was able to keep his mouth shut, but his blood was boiling on the inside.

Michelle noticed. She smiled and thought to herself, *For a person who's mostly listening in, Bill sure looks like he wants to share a few choice words with people.* Michelle took a different approach, however. She found endearing ways to cut through the complaining and self-centered attitude of many people. As a result, she was able to elicit facts.

Three o'clock in the afternoon came quickly. It seemed to creep up on Michelle like a bad guy in a horror film. She arrived at Bill's office. It wasn't much, really. It was like all the other offices at IUI. It was situated on the outside wall of the floor with windows on two walls and the standard, sterile, corporate-painted sheetrock for the other two walls. There was a tidy desk and a small conference table in the room. It looked like a great spot to work until she realized how hot the office was with the afternoon sun beating down on them through the windows.

Michelle and Bill reviewed all the interviews from that day. It was clear that they had uncovered two big pieces of information. First, they had documented the use of over twenty-four systems, spreadsheets, and documents used to capture the "things we say we are going to do." Second, their list of interviewees had grown exponentially.

"I know we've grown, but wow, you don't realize how big a small company can get until you try to talk to almost every employee," Bill said.

"I have no clue what it was like here before, when you old-timers had to walk to work, uphill, both ways, in the snow," Michelle joked. "But yes, we are big. I've now met folks who have worked here longer than I have but I can't recall ever seeing their faces before."

"Well, with all that aside," Bill continued, "I think we can start the document."

Sitting next to Bill at his office conference table, Michelle opened up her *MRIA Outline* document and typed the following:

MRIA

Finding/Concern
– Inconsistent process, ineffective in ensuring security and compliance, resulting in unauthorized and vulnerable software with significant number of defects being released to production.

Current State - Promises (aka "Controls")
– Documented software release process
– Documented software testing process
– [Continue here tomorrow]

"Well, that summarizes everything. Although that just seems like too few words for all the jibber-jabbing, complaining, and real facts we uncovered today," Bill said.

"It's late and I'm too tired to think about how to include anything else. We have copious notes. If we need to, we can always go back to them," Michelle responded.

"Touché, touché," Bill said.

Michelle saved her document and then closed her laptop. It was a couple minutes past five, and she had to get going. Her babysitter got cranky if she had to watch Michelle's twins later than six o'clock.

"I need to leave. I've had enough for the day. Let's pick this back up tomorrow," Michelle suggested.

"Agreed," Bill responded.

Michelle walked back to her cube, grabbed her belongings, and started toward the parking garage. She passed many of the people she'd spoken with earlier. Tossing each one of them a soft smile, she couldn't help but wonder to herself, *IUI has smart and driven people. How could so many things go wrong at a place like this?*

CHAPTER 3

Tuesday, April 5th

The next few days seemed to fly by. Michelle put on her best Sherlock Holmes, with Bill acting as her Dr. Watson. It seemed like there wasn't anyone she didn't speak with. Michelle would have set a meeting with the janitorial staff if she'd thought they had useful insights into how IUI kept promises to external auditors and customers.

Sometimes, it seemed like Michelle's and Bill's back-to-back meetings resembled a cheesy '90s rom-com montage of the first year of a relationship, where everyone is getting along. Everyone is agreeable, energetic, and open. Other times, it resembled one of those serious montages of time spent on computers, debating one another, and burning the midnight oil.

By Tuesday afternoon, the *MRIA Outline* document had grown substantially.

MRIA

Finding/Concern
- Inconsistent process, ineffective in ensuring security and compliance, resulting in unauthorized and vulnerable software with significant number of defects being released to production.

Current State
- Promises (aka "Controls")
    - Documented software release process - Not documented
    - Documented software testing process - Somewhat documented, teams do things differently
- MRAs
    - Insufficient Response - 4
    - Not Responded To - 11
- Main Systems for Process and Documentation
    - Risk - GRC System
    - Security - Knowledge Mgt. Module
    - Server Mgt. System - CMDB

- Product - Ticketing System
- Engineering - Git Repo
- Other Systems
  - Outside of the four main systems, there are 38 other "systems" that consist of community documents and wiki pages but mostly spreadsheets stored all over the company, sometimes on personal computers.
  - See "Appendix - Spreadsheets & Informal Systems" for detailed information and system owners.

Actionable Items
- Based upon the MRAs issued, the following items should be addressed with formal, standardized approaches:
  - Goal
    - Define a minimally acceptable release approach.
  - Objectives
    - Enforce peer reviews of code that is pushed to a production environment.
    - Identify and enforce minimum quality gates.
    - Remove all elevated access to all production environments for everyone.

"It's amazing what happens when you can focus and finish a task, even on a seemingly tight deadline," Bill said.

"I think we talked to everyone," Michelle replied.

"Yes, we did. Everyone, their mother, and their grandparents." Bill studied the document on Michelle's laptop. "This is a solid summary. It's on point for Tim and Carol's request. I think it sets the stage for next actions and solutioning. What do you think?"

"Of course I'm good with it! Condensing all of this information was painful. I feel like there's so much more to say," she replied.

"This isn't really any different than identifying features for a product. Think of all those folks as customers and what we did as requirements analysis," Bill said.

"Oh, that makes sense," said Michelle.

Wednesday, April 6th

"Holy hell!" Jada nearly screamed as she read through the printed version of the *MRIA Outline* document in front of her.

Michelle looked around the room. The expression on the team's faces as they read varied from stunned, shocked, and disappointed to what Michelle could only describe as outright disgusted.

"Forty-two systems . . . " Tim said in disbelief. "This is the type of information Susan needs. Not all of this nitty-gritty," he said, flipping through the appendix sections, "but this first page tells the truth that needs to be told. Even though it hurts looking at this."

"Tim, to make the most of this meeting, let's discuss the *Actionable Items* listed here. Information like this is key to the IUI response to the MRIA," Jada said.

"Okay, great," said Tim. "Let's start with the goal: *Define a minimally acceptable release approach.*"

"We've made great strides toward this in our DevOps journey, but we still have some gaps, particularly in digital banking," said Michelle, looking at Carol. "Developers tend to use workarounds in legacy back end processes. Our documentation is either nonexistent or unclear. Developers who know the process follow it. But those who don't know the process blame problems on legacy systems and the older applications developers who were here before our DevOps journey.

"It's further complicated by the subjective nature of how we create evidence. For example, all the evidence is implicitly defined in our CMDB[1] system without any hard or objective evidence being stored anywhere. Tim's team runs reports against that CMDB system."

"Yes," said Tim. "And for the most part we believe we're in compliance. But we don't actually validate the data."

"Why not?" asked Jada. No answer was forthcoming.

"Okay, what's next, Michelle?" asked Tim.

"We lack code reviews before deployments. It seems everyone thinks everyone else is doing this correctly, but not everyone is." Michelle laughed, failing to conceal the irony. She then continued. "There are a number of ways to bypass this process."

"Like what?" asked Jada.

"Oh, I remember this one," Bill jumped in. "Wasn't there someone on one of your teams, Michelle, who built an automated script to auto-review his own work using a service account?"

"Say what?" Jada said, surprise evident in her voice. "And then what happened?"

Michelle replied, "We took his service account away. He left IUI last year. He came from a start-up and didn't actually like our way of working . . . forget it. Let's continue."

"It's actually really frightening to see that we have wide-open gaps," said Tim.

---

1 CMDB stands for configuration management database.

"One of the issues is that we don't have a formal way to request a peer review. Basically, a person committing code has to track someone down and literally ask them to stop what they're doing to help them with the review. That is, if anyone bothers to do it. It's disruptive, slow, inconsistent, and unreliable. We don't allow for proper structure or bandwidth to support a formalized process for code reviews," said Michelle.

"But, if you ask me what makes me nervous . . . we have too many old open-source and commercial libraries and packages. We've been using these libraries for so long that nobody pays any attention to them. They're likely full of vulnerabilities and in need of patches. Heck, we don't even know if we're using correctly licensed third-party software."

"That is bad," said Tim, frowning.

"But what's even worse," Michelle continued, "is that there's no consistent evidence of the security controls that Audit can easily examine. Some teams manually enter findings into their development backlog for remediation and others pass around PDF files or spreadsheets to their leaders. It's completely scattershot."

"And there's still more?" asked Jada, with a hollow laugh.

"Oh, yes," said Tim, wide-eyed, looking first at Jada and then the rest of the team. "I have heard that we lack controls, or tollgates, within the release pipelines. When Engineering teams started implementing automated pipelines, I was told that they would put some basic control gates in there. But I guess it never happened."[2]

"Unfortunately, Tim is correct," said Michelle, shaking her head. "Over time, teams have been creating workarounds and getting exceptions to bypass the toll-gates. As we've grown, so has our number of pipelines. It's made it really hard to manage what happens in each one. In fact, many delivery teams have access to the CI/CD tools but have actually turned these controls off."

"What?" said Jada, looking as if she had just witnessed someone running a red light in front of her. "How did that happen?!"

"Well, it looks like it started with just a few exceptions when there was pressure to deliver at a certain time and we couldn't afford to delay the release. In time, though, it appears our system has become the 'normalization of deviance,'" Michelle said, physically making the quote marks with her hands as she said it.

"Huh? The what of what?" someone in the back of the room asked.

"Diane Vaughan wrote a book called *The Challenger Launch Decision*. The whole *Challenger* disaster happened because deviance from correct or proper behavior became normalized in the US space program. It's actually very common in corporate culture, and, well . . ." Michelle suddenly looked a little sheepish, "it's happening here."

---

2. See Appendix 2 for more on pipelines.

"Great," Jada sighed.

"And finally . . ." said Michelle, adjusting her glasses.

"Thank goodness!" said Jada, rolling her eyes.

"We have a very serious finding related to elevated access."

"Like the other findings weren't all that serious," Tim smirked. A laugh rippled around the room.

Michelle calmly carried on. "The Development and Operations teams have a way to bypass the process. Basically, there are too many incidents of 'break-glass'[3] access to systems. No one follows the guidelines. Team leads and managers grant approval left and right. I don't think that the break-glass system even works."

"But we have clear and published guidelines for this," said Tim.

"I know," said Michelle. "But people just ignore them. We don't have a way to track elevated access requests. Our system has been open to abuse. And," she added, taking a sip of her water, "it appears it has been abused."

"This is worse than I thought," Jada said. "We have to maintain segregation of duties. We'll never receive a favorable examination with the regulators without it. Do I need to remind everyone in this room about Enron?!" Jada threw up her hands and looked around. There was silence. Michelle noticed a lot of people suddenly looking down into their laps. Throwing the name Enron around a bank was a surefire way to get people really uncomfortable really fast.

"Well," Michelle piped up. "Actually, that should be achieved simply enough through the peer review system."

"No way. We can't have a developer pushing their own code into production and still achieve segregation of duties," Jada clarified. "We'll have to show that no one has both 'developer' and 'operations' roles. And the developer role cannot deploy to production. We also need to have a way to generate reports and compare the list of 'developers' against the list of 'operations' to ensure there is no overlap. We need to do that at least once every quarter."

Michelle quickly interjected. "But Jada, we don't have two roles anymore, not in the teams that have been 'DevOps-ified.' Now everyone is a developer. We're either writing code for features or writing code for infrastructure. It's all software now."

"What?" Jada stood up, looking furious. "When did that happen? Who made that decision? Why was I not consulted?"

---

3. The concept of "break glass" (which draws its name from breaking the glass to pull a fire alarm) refers to an easy and quick way for a person who does not have access privileges to perform certain functions or obtain information to gain that access when necessary. A good "break glass" process should be well-documented and understood. It should provide a secure and auditable log, as well as notify and alert the governance and leadership team of actions taken. "Break glass" events should be an exceptional process, rarely needed or followed.

Tim leaned forward and commented sarcastically, "That was our DevOps transformation. The one we've been on for the last few years. Everybody said put Dev and Ops together, and that's what we did. We made everyone a full-stack developer and put everyone in a single role: developer."

Michelle sensed that the discussion was going downhill. She stood up and firmly said, "Listen, I was in a Lean Coffee session[4] at a DevOps conference last year. The topic on my table was exactly this, segregation of duties. There were at least fifteen people at my table who were from other banks, retailers, software companies, and FinTech startups, even some folks from that famous auto parts manufacturer, Parts Unlimited. Everyone agreed unequivocally that segregation of duties is a joke. It doesn't work."

Michelle paused for a second to judge Jada's and Tim's reactions before continuing. "We assume that just because the code deployer belongs to another role, there will be no risk, or less risk. We've all seen the movie *Office Space*! Haven't we?"

There were rumbles of acknowledgment from all corners of the room.

"Well, everyone at my table felt that segregation of duties presents an increased risk that someone not familiar with the change is actually putting the change in production!" Michelle looked at Jada. "And if you talk about a 'bad actor' scenario, an ops engineer can cause equal or greater damage than a developer."

Jada quickly interjected. "So how do you ensure that no single developer has the ability to make a code change and deploy to production without anyone else's knowledge? After all, that is the actual risk that we need to mitigate—and convince the regulators that we have it mitigated."

"Exactly!" Michelle felt a lot better now. They were back on the same page, she hoped. "We have much better ways to mitigate that risk. We have all our application code in Git repositories. We use a CI/CD pipeline to build and deploy code all the way to production. Our pipeline is nothing but a set of codified build and deployment workflows, and we store them in the same Git repository, along with our infrastructure code. Now, if we take away elevated production access from every developer and *ensure* that every code change is peer reviewed before production deployment, we will have the best way to mitigate that risk that you mentioned, Jada. The key is enforcing the peer review process."

"So," Tim said, stopping Jada before she could respond. "Do we do any of that now?"

Michelle looked away and said, "No." Lowering her voice and sounding a lot less energetic, she continued. "I mean, I know that most teams have pipelines and infra-

---

4. Lean Coffee is a structured, agenda-less style of meeting where participants vote on the subject(s) to be discussed and when to move on to the next subject. You can learn more in the book *Making Work Visible* by Dominica DeGrandis.

structure code in their repositories. But that's about it. And as I was saying earlier, our peer review process is broken too."

Tim looked at Bill and said, "I think we all understand the extent and nature of the problem. Let's talk about roles. Bill, as Product Manager, you have ultimate accountability for digital banking."

Bill had sat through the discussion quietly, watching the room. As Michelle had gone through the findings, he'd observed Tim and Jada's reactions. The situation that IUI had found itself in was finally starting to sink in, and he was feeling fearful.

"Yes, but am I the right owner for this? These aren't features. These are security and compliance issues. Engineering problems." There were murmurs of agreement from many in the room. A voice in Bill's head wondered what his security and compliance colleagues did besides tell him what he was doing wrong. He glanced at Michelle's face. It was evident that she didn't intend to take ownership of these problems.

"But," said Tim, "one could look at compliance and security features as non-functional requirements in a product, right? If a security hole gets exploited or a compliance control is not met, that means the software has a bug or undocumented feature. And you don't like those, do you, Bill?"

"No," said Bill. "I really don't. Michelle and I actually had this conversation just the other day. She was quoting a guy . . . James . . . "

"James Wickett," said Michelle, smiling.

"That's it. You heard him talk at a DevOps Enterprise Summit session on security bugs. He said: 'A bug is a bug is a bug.'[5] That's right, isn't it, Michelle?"

"Yup," Michelle nodded.

"You know, as Product Manager, it's my job to ensure a product's features meet market needs. And we do that. We deliver a lot. Quarter after quarter we've met and exceeded expectations. But with all that output, I'm wondering what actual outcomes we drove. I'm wondering if we created a build trap.[6]"

"What's that?" asked Tim.

"It's something I've read about recently," said Bill. "It's a concept where if you only focus on delivering features and neglect experimentation and learning, than you likely aren't building the right thing; moreover, you're not learning or improving how you're building, which is our case here. We never put stories in to improve and possibly re-architect our build process for complete traceability and compliance. This is all about shifting left on security, quality, and resiliency."

---

5. Learn more in the 2017 DevOps Enterprise Summit presentation by James Wickett, "Lightning Talk: Security is in Crisis, A New Journey Begins," at https://videolibrary.doesvirtual.com/?video =524054897.

6 Learn more about the concept of a build trap in *Escaping the Build Trap: How Effective Product Management Creates Real Value* by Melissa Perri.

Bill's revelation seemed to land well in the room. Everyone looked at Bill, then at each other. They all started to realize how these MRAs could have been ignored for so long. Everyone was so busy trying to *keep up* with daily work that they had no time to *improve* daily work. That included security, quality, and resiliency.

Bill continued, "To do this the right way, we're going to have to bring in several teams from the business. And you know those teams will likely refuse to change how they work. This isn't their process. It's not going to be easy to get this new idea through those silos. But I think I know how to have this discussion with stakeholders. They will sometimes need to wait a little longer for a product. We can't maintain a 'move fast and break things' culture if it means we end up in a mess like we're finding ourselves in today. But I still wonder, if this is a security and compliance problem, shouldn't it be owned by Risk?" He looked at Jada.

"We'll be right there with you," said Jada. "But it's your product. You should own the features. And, as Tim said and you agreed, this is a feature. We're going to have to learn to collaborate better and create a pattern of working for the rest of the organization to learn from. I don't think we've ever done this together before."

Tim agreed. "Jada, we'll need to include members from my Security teams and your Risk teams to participate in this project. I'm guessing Barry and Andrea are key people we should have working on this because . . . ?"

Jada nodded. "I'll get us a meeting set up."

"Okay, it sounds like we should treat this like a market problem," Bill said, though he still felt a little uneasy about it. "We'll need their expertise to understand what I've been missing when planning a product. And I'd like Michelle to help drive an engineering solution."

"Sure," Michelle responded. She had been surprised at how well she and Bill had worked together over the last week. And after listening to everyone's pain points and problems, she was eager to begin crafting a solution.

"Okay, I think we all know what to do next!" Tim exclaimed. "I'll take what we've decided here today to Susan at the huddle tomorrow. Then we'll reconvene in a week to share what headway we've made. Let's do this like we did today and have all the material ready before Susan's weekly huddle. Michelle, I'll set up a kick-off time with you."

"Sound great," Michelle replied.

CHAPTER 4

Wednesday, April 6th *(continued)*

The room emptied fast, but Bill stayed behind. He sat in his chair, contemplating the position he'd just put himself in: right in front of the firing line. This wasn't going to be easy. The thought of managing upward, sideways, and downward made him dizzy and uncertain. He pondered the next steps.

He needed to think. He packed up his stuff and tidied the chairs as he left the room, planning to have a beer over lunch at the local pub. The thought of an afternoon stout and some Cypress Point raw oysters made him happy.

On the way down the hall, he passed Susan's office. As he walked briskly past her door, he could see someone presenting to her.

For a CEO in a highly regulated company, Susan was pretty open. She lived the company values by never shutting her door unless it was absolutely required. Many folks were polite enough not to bother her when someone else was in the office, but it was generally accepted that you could if you needed to.

Bill's attention was grabbed by a slide that was projected on the wall monitor. Susan was reviewing it with a bespectacled man, Jason Colbert, the SVP of Digital Transformation. Jason had been brought in to lead the continued DevOps transformation of IUI a year ago, and they had just started working together on a new digital product strategy.

Jason was waxing eloquently about his presentation. There wasn't any formal style to this slide, just white words in bold, simple type on a charcoal background. The words read "DevOps failed you." It grabbed him.

Bill couldn't hear clearly what Jason was saying. He walked closer to the door and waited to see if he could make out anything.

He gave it a couple more seconds, turned around, and then walked past the door again.

That slide was really intriguing to him. No one else from IT was in the room. And why was DevOps under fire? They were one of the few firms he knew of that had successfully transformed from an outdated "Plan, Build, Run" siloed way of working to a more collaborative, product-focused approach. IUI was among the first few companies that participated in DORA metrics.[1] Why was the head of IUI's digital transformation now suggesting that DevOps had failed?

Finally he caught a snippet of the conversation.

"DevOps failed you. But it wasn't DevOps' fault. Most people forget to apply systems thinking to their DevOps transformation. In fact, Jabe Bloom has some great blogs on this you should check out. He calls it the 'Three Economies.'[2]

"You've probably heard the term 'DevSecOps'[3] thrown around these days," Jason continued. "It's not just another buzzword; it's an admission that there is more to DevOps than just Dev and Ops. An organization must go beyond developers and operations. They must consider everyone in the value stream."

Susan was looking at Jason very seriously. Bill could only imagine the stress she was under and the pressure she was getting from the board with this MRIA.

Before Bill realized he was staring, Susan looked directly at him and smiled.

"Hey, Bill, come on in."

Bill jumped at the sound of her voice.

That dizzy feeling came back to him. His palms began to sweat. He was very uncomfortable knowing he'd been caught like a child hiding on the stairs peeking between the banisters and listening in on his parents' conversation way past bedtime. He decided to style it out.

"Sorry for the office creeping," he began. "I saw the words 'DevOps failed you' and I couldn't help myself."

Susan smiled broadly. Jason turned around to face Bill, a jovial grin on his face. This wasn't what he expected. From the tone of the conversation he had overheard, it sounded like they were discussing a dire situation. But now Jason and Susan were both all smiles.

"Yes, Jason was just teaching me a thing or two about how to build better software," Susan said. "Can you imagine that. A CEO learning about building software."

"Hiya, Bill!" Jason said with enthusiasm. "What can I say? I'm a recovering academic and sometimes I get a chance to practice my old trade. Susan is kind enough to let me chew on her ear from time to time. We were just discussing the audit findings, and I was sharing some observations and insights."

Jason always had an excited yet relaxed tone. Today he wore wrinkled khaki pants and an untucked denim button-down shirt. He seemed jolly and talked as if

---

1 DevOps Research & Assessment (DORA) is responsible for the annual *State of DevOps Reports*. Their research was also the basis for the book *Accelerate* by Dr. Nicole Forsgren, Jez Humble, and Gene Kim. https://www.devops-research.com/research.html.

2. Read more on the concept of three economies in this blog from Jabe Bloom: http://blog.jabebloom. com/2020/03/04/the-three-economies-an-introduction/.

3. See Appendix 3 to learn more about DevSecOps and the DevSecOps Manifesto.

he'd just stuck his hand in the honey pot and was licking away. Definitely not what Bill thought of as a typical Boston academic.

"By the way," Jason said to Bill, "we have a couple of Sicilian cannoli left over from Bova's Bakery. Best cannoli west of the Atlantic, you know." He nodded at the pastries, and Bill grabbed one gratefully. The oysters could wait.

"I was just telling Susan how DevOps ideals are great, but they're rooted in the core chronic conflict between Development and Operations," Jason said, turning back to Susan. "'Core chronic conflict' is a fancy way of saying that people across the organization are incentivized in ways that prevent cooperation, therefore preventing the achievement of organization-wide goals. This has directly led to the mess IUI is finding itself in today with the MRIA."

"Our incentives are causing these problems? How?" Susan had lost her smile and was once again listening to Jason with a serious look on her face. It made Bill feel the weight that she obviously had on her shoulders. He took a bite of his cannoli and sat on the edge of her desk, listening closely as Jason explained.

"Developers are incentivized to go faster, delivering more features quickly."

Bill nodded while taking another bite of his cannoli.

"Operations," Jason continued, "are incentivized to reduce risk of change. If you're delivering features quickly, you're changing at a fast pace. Therefore there is a core chronic conflict between Development and Operations. Moving quickly versus the risk of change."

"Yes, I think we were just coming to a similar finding during our MRIA meeting a few minutes ago," Bill said.

Susan turned toward him, and he suddenly felt like he'd put himself on the spot. "We were looking at how Development might have inadvertently become a build trap," he continued. "Paving at least part of the path to the mess we're in now."

"That's certainly part of the problem," Jason added before turning back to Susan. "When it comes to the audit findings, I think it comes around to the fact that the Security, Risk, and Compliance folks are trained and incentivized to think of every possible way a bad actor could compromise your system. Susan, I'll send you a copy of the book Bill's referring to."

Susan nodded her appreciation.

"Josh Corman, a famous security specialist," Jason continued, "says software's not eating the world, as has been famously said; it's infecting the world.[4] Not that creating a lot of new software is a bad thing! It's just that we're constantly creating new opportunities for security compromises. Every time you add a new feature," he said, looking pointedly at Bill, "these folks assess if the change created a compromise.

---

4. You can watch the Josh Corman presentation from LISA15 here: https://www.youtube.com/watch?v=jkoFL7hGiUk&t=1s.

"It's another core chronic conflict: developers are incentivized to regularly intro- duce features—the build trap you spoke of—and Security, Risk, and Compliance are incentivized to minimize the likelihood or impact of all known possibilities, which can take time if not done well, creating a problem for the developers' need to move fast, and so it goes around and around . . ."

He trailed off, lost in a vivid recollection that had come to him. Finally he came back to earth. "Sometimes the actual language that the Security folks use can be blunt," Jason joked. "I blame it on their vendors. So alarmist!" he chuckled.

Bill chewed on the revelation Jason shared. On the face of it, Bill felt this was obvious. He knew this was a big issue, but as far as he was concerned, it had always been this way, and he saw no prospect of it changing. Or could it? Hadn't they already done just this sort of change with DevOps, like Jason said?

Susan looked at Jason. "So we need to think about how we DevOps-ify Security, Risk, and Compliance?"

"Exactamundo!" Jason said. "What IUI has been able to achieve with DevOps is great, but it's not enough. And this MRIA brings to light exactly what we need to shift left next. I've been watching other organizations try to handle these types of issues. Some are treating security and compliance as if it's a feature of their product."

"Hold on, did you say 'treat security and compliance as if it was a feature'?"

"Yup," Jason nodded.

Bill was surprised, but hearing the words mirrored back to him pushed his creeping panic attack away. It was replaced with cartoon scenes of bluebirds singing, bunnies hopping, and flowers blooming. He felt a smile appear on his face.

"We just said the same thing in my meeting with Tim and Jada," Bill replied. "In fact," he said, turning toward Susan, "they'll likely be filling you in on just that at the huddle tomorrow."

"I guess great minds think alike," Susan chuckled.

"I'm not sure if it's great minds or more software common sense these days," Jason stated. "Take *The DevOps Handbook*. It points out three key aspects of DevOps: flow, feedback, and continuous learning."

"Yeah, the three ways," said Bill.

"You betcha. Well, those same concepts can be applied to Security, Compliance, Risk, and any other stakeholder along a value stream. These days, I'd argue that Development versus Operations is mostly solved. Now it's all about systematically looking at all other parties that ensure the quality of software and including them in our shift-left mentality."

"'Shift-left mentality'?[5] You've said that a couple of times. Can you explain that more?" Susan asked.

---

5. See Appendix 4 for more on the concept of "shift left."

"Sure. Shifting left is a technique for bringing software testing as far forward as possible in the software requirements and design process. Imagine a diagram of the steps in the process. Testing typically happens after several other things and sits on the right-hand side of the picture. By moving it earlier in the process, we shift it left. Have you heard your developers talk about test-driven design and development?" Jason asked, turning toward Bill for confirmation.

"Oh yeah, TDD is one of Michelle's favorite soapboxes," Bill recalled.

"Good—that's an important soapbox. When you shift things left, they become a forethought in the software design and development process, not an afterthought. Think of Security, Compliance, and Risk as a form of testing," Jason explained, looking at Susan and Bill in turn. "Shift-left testing makes people think about how the software is supposed to operate, and then they codify tests. Then, once the tests are created, the engineers build the product and automatically run the tests to see if the product passes the tests. Testing this way is like creating a blueprint.

"If you watch how cars are built, before any car is produced, a blueprint for all components is designed. That blueprint is the specification for how the car operates. Testing functions that way as well, and so should Security, Compliance, and Risk."

"To be clear, you're saying we need to start baking Security, Compliance, and Risk into the upfront software designs?" Bill asked.

"That's right! Just like testing, shifting security left allows it to be codified and automatically validated as the software is built. If it's done correctly, the only human touch the software experiences, besides an end-user, is the smart people defining the tests, the smart people codifying the security and compliance policies, and the smart people writing the software. No longer do we need to have smart people performing audits by manually checking screenshots to validate things are all good.

"Actually, that reminds me of a story I heard from a colleague at another company that shall not be named," he said, placing a finger over his lips. "She found out that one of their teams had been uploading the same screenshot as testing evidence for sixteen months!"

"Oh, please tell me that's not happening here," Susan said over Jason's laughs.

Bill was profoundly affected by this insight. It all made so much sense to him, but the problem was implementation. How were they going to actually make these changes? Why had no one talked about this before?

"As a product owner, I can prioritize security and compliance as features of my product," Bill said. "If I challenge the team to shift these actions left as a means of validating the software, maybe I can help ensure we reduce audit findings. But the findings were about the software release process. I can't change how they build software, can I?"

"Bill has a point. What do you think, Jason?" Susan said.

"Their processes reflect how you incentivize them. If you prioritize not just features but also how the features are brought to market, you give the organization a reason and the power to change the way software development is done. Most leaders and managers in digital native companies get this. They get this so well that you won't hear them talk about DevOps or anything like what we're talking about. They'll just tell you that's how they've always worked."

Jason stood up for a second and did a little stretch.

"Bill, why don't you find out what Security and Compliance needs, then work with the engineers to codify these needs into your software as if it were a feature?"

"It sounds like a good plan in theory, but I still wonder why Jada's team doesn't do this?" Bill asked.

Susan responded with a serious face. "Bill, I don't know everything about software development, but I do know that IUI is not a digital native, and therefore change has to be made. You're the person with a P&L incentive to see the change. You're the person with the opportunity to shepherd the change and help lead Jada's organization through the change."

"So, where do you think you should start?" Jason asked, looking at Bill the way his college professor used to stare at the class when she presented them with an impossible challenge.

"Well, let's see . . . " Bill felt like he was standing at the edge of a cliff.

"We've been talking about treating this like a product," Jason offered. "How would you bring a product to market when you have no objective evidence the market wants it but some qualitative evidence that it's desired?"

Bill mused out loud, feeling slightly more comfortable. "I would create small, quick experiments, minimally viable products, to see what does and does not work," Bill offered. Yeah, he knew how to do that. He and his team did it all the time.

Jason smiled. "I think you've got it. But here," Jason said as he walked over to Susan's desk. Bill was a little amazed as he watched Jason riffle through her drawers, pulling out a pen and pad of paper. "I recently read a couple of documents that I think might help you and the Engineering team on your journey." He jotted down some notes.

Jason walked back over to Bill, handing him the piece of paper.

"Now, those cannoli were a good start, but I'm hungry," Jason said, turning to Susan. "Where can we get something more substantial to eat?"

CHAPTER 5

Tuesday, April 19th

Bill sat at his desk, staring out the window. It had been a long couple weeks since he stood in Susan's office looking at the "DevOps has failed you" slide with Jason. Since then, he'd looked up the resources Jason had scribbled for him on that scrap of paper. They had turned out to be a couple of guidance papers. The first was short and simple, but it was powerful.

Dear Auditor[1] was a simple letter written by an imaginary engineering team to their auditor colleagues. Reading it had made Bill realize just how much blame he and many others at IUI always placed on the Audit team. They seemed like the easy scapegoats they could throw all their woes at. But it had become clear that IUI was never going to drag itself out of this mess without seeing Audit in a new light.

He had immediately forwarded the letter to Michelle, who shared it with her Engineering team. They were hard at work trying to build a solution to their predicament. The team nicknamed themselves "the Kraken"—a play on Liam Neeson's famous line "Release the kraken!" from the 2010 movie *Clash of the Titans*.

Along the way, Michelle and her team realized they had to tackle their own perceptions and mindsets. They had even drafted their own version of the *Dear Auditor* letter and shared it with the whole company. They felt like this letter was a great way to set the tone for a fundamental change in how IUI's Engineering and Audit groups operated, working together as a team instead of adversaries. They knew it wouldn't change anything overnight, but they hoped it was a beginning.

Dear Auditor,

We realize that we have been rapidly changing our practices from Agile and DevOps to cloud and containers. Yes, we have been busy, and we are having great success delivering faster than ever with better quality, responding competitively to market pressures. However, this approach isn't just icing on the cake. The only

---

1. Visit http://dearauditor.org/ to read the original *Dear Auditor* paper.

sustainable advantage in our industry is the ability to meet customer demands faster and more reliably than our competitors.

But with all this growth, we made a tragic mistake: we forgot to bring you along for the ride. That is totally our fault, and we want to make it right. We are going to make some new commitments, including the following:

- We will bring you along.
- We will be fully transparent with you about our development process.
- We realize that we own the risks of our business, and we will act accordingly.
- We will maintain an open channel of discussion to demonstrate to you how we manage risks with our modern development practices.

For example, you have told us that you are concerned about the separation of duties in Agile and DevOps practices, and we heard you! We have a better way to manage this issue now. Maintaining version control for everything we work on, enforcing peer review for all changes, releasing via a secure pipeline, restricting production access, and monitoring unauthorized changes in production systems are being enacted to help address your concern.

The DevOps community has been experimenting quite a bit over the last several years, and common practice now represents the collective wisdom across many companies, industries, and countries.

We have compiled a list of Audit concerns and documented them in a Risk Control Matrix with details about the controls, our practices, and evidence that has been collected to support each control. We hope this matrix provides a way for us to collaborate on risk mitigation practices from now on.

We stand by our commitment to providing value at a fast pace. We are regrouping in order to improve our processes with you, and we are truly excited to move forward together.

—The Kraken Team

Bill spun in his chair to look at the letter, which he had printed out and pinned to his wall along with a calendar ticking down the days until they had to respond to the MRIA. Alongside it was a picture taken at the last company-wide forum. The picture was no more than a sea of faces, but it, along with the letter and calendar, acted as his motivation. He and the team had to fix their governance issues before the deadline set by the MRIA. If they didn't, everyone in that sea of faces would be unemployed. Not to mention the stakeholders they'd be letting down. Bill wasn't sure how he'd be able to handle facing that kind of failure.

"It seems to be getting a lot of traction," Michelle said from the doorway.

Bill, startled slightly, spun around to look at her. She was pointing at the letter he had been staring at.

"Yes, but it's not a solution that we can pick up and run with. We still have a long way to go."

Even though she had a slight smile on her face, Bill had been working closely with Michelle for long enough now that he could see there was something troubling her. It had been a hard few weeks discovering the extent of the mess they were in. He wasn't sure if they'd be able to unravel the complex knot of requirements and systems, but he hoped the second resource Jason had given him would help the team unlock something.

"Everyone's gathered together. You ready?" Michelle asked.

"Ready." Bill grabbed his tablet and followed Michelle down the hall to one of the larger conference rooms. It was packed with the Engineering team tasked with helping Michelle. The seriousness of the MRIA meant they were able to assemble a special task force to focus on just this problem. At least, that was the intention. He'd be beyond surprised if they were able to make it to the end without someone getting pulled off to help with some crisis or another.

Michelle and the team were an eclectic mix of engineers. Some had bounced around different companies in the area. Others, like Michelle, were starting to make a career for themselves at IUI.

One notable team member was Omar. He wasn't the most senior engineer on the team, but he was, like Michelle, a natural leader. Others tended to rally around him when they needed to solve difficult technical problems.

Omar had joined IUI three years ago and was not shy about sharing his opinion. He often jumped at a problem as though it was easily solvable only to realize later that it was far more complex than he had imagined. But when he saw the complexity, he just dug into it deeper and wouldn't stop until it was fixed. Michelle welcomed his fearless attitude for this effort.

In addition to the Engineering team, Jada and Tim had requested people in their organizations to be part of the design process: Andrea from Audit and Barry from Security.

Andrea had started at IUI about six years ago. She never intended to have a career as an internal auditor; it had just played out that way. Andrea had worked her way up from a bank clerk to her current position. She was one of the few people at IUI who had taken advantage of the cross-training opportunities they offered. She found enjoyment in the audit process. She liked her house neat and tidy, and auditing made her feel like she was keeping the business neat and tidy too.

Barry, on the other hand, was curmudgeonly and stubborn. A director under Tim, he was selected for two reasons. First, for all of Barry's gruff demeanor, he was the most forward-thinking security professional IUI had. Second, Barry needed to be stretched. His management had noticed lately that he was starting to just coast. Barry's manager wanted to give him something more challenging. They couldn't tell if Barry was being lazy or if their asks were making him bored.

"Has everyone had a chance to read the *DevOps Automated Governance Reference Architecture*[2] document that Michelle and I shared with you?"

"Yes, it was duller than a butter knife," Barry said curtly.

"Really? I felt like the authors knew our release management approach intimately," Omar observed. "They wrote about how to make it better in many ways I'd never thought about before."

Andrea interjected. "The framework they used to identify the inputs, outputs, risk, controls, actors, and actions was very clear. But I don't understand things like build or dependency management. Though, even without that context, that paper laid out a good approach to ensuring that whatever happens in those process boxes, the outcome is clearly auditable."

"I agree," Bill said. "What I found most interesting was how this automated process could help solve our problem of delivery velocity. I think we can all agree that as IUI has grown, our rate of delivery has increased quite substantially. It has become very difficult for us to stay in compliance with our own security and compliance requirements without slowing down."

"Exactly," Michelle added. "It's not that the developers want to do the wrong thing. They're not actively trying to break the system."

"You could have fooled me," Barry replied.

"But when it's so hard to stay in compliance," she continued, "when the road is full of potholes and obstacles, well, we've had to find ways around those so that we could still meet our delivery requirements."

"I had a similar discussion not too long ago with Jason. Jason was explaining that our incentives are causing these problems. Developers are incentivized to go faster, delivering more features quickly, and I've been supporting that. Ops, Security, and Audit," Bill said, nodding at Barry and Andrea, "well, you all have been incentivized to reduce risk, of course. Which in our old system slowed things down so that Dev couldn't ship features quickly. It's a conflict. I think Jason called it a core chronic conflict."

"Talk about a merry-go-round of doom," Michelle said, chuckling. Andrea smiled back at her, but Barry didn't look at all amused. "Uh, let's get back to this paper. The DevOps journey we've been on has helped Dev automate more and more

---

2. The original *DevOps Automated Governance Reference Architecture* paper was written by Michael Nygard, Tapabrata Pal, Stephen Magill, Sam Guckenheimer, John Willis, John Rzeszotarski, Dwayne Holmes, Courtney Kissler, Dan Beauregard, and Colette Tauscher in 2019. You can read it here: ITRevolution.com/resources.

practices, moving faster and faster. And, well, like the 'Dear Auditor' letter showed, we've left you all behind. But it doesn't have to stay that way. This paper shows we can *automate* governance! I mean, how wild and exciting is that!"

"Totally!" Omar agreed. "This paper shows how we can implement an automated process to track all the governance requirements throughout the delivery pipeline. It's wild!"

"I think this could really be the answer to our problem," Michelle responded. "I mean, we have no choice other than automating our software delivery governance anyway. We're not going back in time."

"This is great enthusiasm," Bill said. "But I want to make sure we are baselined on the problem we need to solve. In the MRIA Outline document Michelle and I have shared with you all, we are focused on designing an approach for the actionable items. It's important to remember that the approach we choose needs to provide a paved road. That is, an easy, or at least easier, path for Dev to follow."

"Yeah, otherwise developers are going to feel like they're just getting hit with a boatload of new policies that will make meeting their incentive of fast delivery even harder. And then they'll continue to find more workarounds, and we'll still be out of compliance. We'll still be in the same mess we're in right now." Michelle took a deep breath. She looked back down at the printed MRIA Outline doc. "So, the actionable items are:

Actionable Items

- Based upon the MRAs issued, the following items should be addressed
  with formal standardized approaches:
    - Goal: Define a minimally acceptable release approach
    - Objectives
      - Enforce peer reviews of code that is pushed to a production environment.
      - Identify and enforce minimum quality gates.
      - Remove all elevated access to all production environments for everyone.

"I see why we're in this mess. You all haven't the slightest clue how to keep your house in order," Barry blurted out.

"Who left surprises in your cereal this morning?" Omar responded. He wasn't having any of Barry's attitude.

"Michelle, are you saying we need to replace our pipelines?" Bill inquired, ignoring Omar.

"No, we're not trying to replace the delivery pipeline. To meet the MRIA, we need to have a documented approach. That's first. Second, we want to bring in this automated governance approach, which is about *augmenting* existing pipelines and tool chains," Michelle explained. "The original DevOps ideals addressed the disconnect between development and operations. It didn't consider the roles of Security, Compliance, Risk, and Audit. So we're just trying to bring you all into the fold, all without having to slow down."

She picked up her tablet and continued. "Turn to page eight of *DevOps Automated Governance Reference Architecture*. I think this could be the baseline for our documented minimally acceptable release approach."

Michelle projected her tablet onto the screen at the front of the conference room.

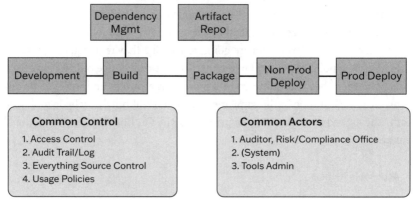

* Source: *DevOps Automated Governance Reference Architecture*

"That has nothing to do with security," Barry commented.

"Barry, it's a baseline," Michelle responded. "We need to build upon it. Do you have recommendations for injecting security considerations into this?"

Barry paused for a moment. "I wasn't brought here for this."

"Yes, you were," interjected Bill. "The design of our new approach includes security and auditing concerns. Our goal is to shift these aspects of the software delivery process left. You're an expert regarding security concerns. Security in our process is not an option. Your involvement may be. Should you and I speak with Tim about finding someone more willing to help?"

The room fell silent. Barry sat there, stone-faced and emotionless, not even appearing to think about what Bill just said.

"Okay, I apologize. That's not necessary," Barry started. He looked back at the screen, obviously in thought. He was silent for a few minutes before adding, "I may have a couple ideas. Let's continue and I'll get back to you all."

Bill smiled, sensing he'd won the battle. "Okay, looking forward to your input."

Michelle, pleased to have some of the tension eased, pointed to the screen. "So this is our generic pipeline. Our teams develop code, automatically build the target executable while pulling down various dependencies from the dependency management system, package the necessary files together, and publish the package into our artifact repository. Next step in the pipeline is to deploy the package to non-production environments . . ."

Barry interjected "Do we not test what we write?"

Michelle answered, "As I was saying, this is a baseline . . . of course we test, and that's why we deploy to a non-production environment first. We test there, and if everything looks okay, we finally deploy to production. We have some common controls across the pipeline stages and the tools that we use. We also have controls around who gets access to our tools and how they access each tool's features. We have audit logs . . . are you all following me?" Michelle looked around.

Everyone was looking at her and waiting.

"Okay good." She smiled and continued. "Our digital team has every pipeline code in our source control tool. So next, we need to talk about how we show evidence of our actionable items."

Michelle projected a new image onto the screen. "Here is a simple table outlining a basic set of attestations. And by 'attestations,' I mean our claims of how we're meeting these controls."

Action Items	Control Stage	Attestation	Source of Truth	Example
Peer Review	Build	Number of Approvers	Source Control Tool	Pass
Controls/ Tollgates	Deployment	Pass/Fail	Policy Engine	Pass
Elevated Access	Deployment	Pass/Fail	Policy Engine	Pass

"Bill and I went down the rabbit hole a couple times trying to think of everything. Then we realized we were just spinning our wheels. These seem like a good place to start."

"Have you considered where you'll get the evidence and how we'll collect it? And how do we apply policies?" Andrea inquired.

"Yes, that was part of our Wonderland excursion during discovery these past few weeks. That's why this team is here. Let's structure an approach to answer the same questions you asked, Andrea," Michelle responded.

"What about the tools or systems to automate this?" Omar asked next.

"We talked about that, but not much. If we start with a tool-first approach, we may miss the forest for the trees. I think it's best if we design the business process of automated governance first and then do a tool and technologies selection."

"What?! We can accomplish much more if we just pick some tools and go," Omar challenged.

"No offense, Omar, but that comment right there is how we got into this mess. If we couple ourselves to the implementation—if we just do what the tools can do— than we will always be limited to the capabilities of our tools. What happens if we need a capability that the tool doesn't offer?" Michelle replied.

"We build a tool and integrate it," Omar responded quickly, as if it were the only truth.

"Omar, I think you're missing the point. I can get with you later to talk about architecture versus implementation. Implementation first is akin to the tail wagging the dog," Michelle said as a means to end the distracting conversation.

"Michelle, you're talking about starting with business architecture, correct?" Andrea asked.

"Yes! No offense, but I'm surprised you've heard about that," Michelle responded.

"Don't mistake me for anyone who knows more than those two words," Andrea quipped. "One of IT's enterprise architects had training on some open group framework thing. All I remember was their incessant repetition of 'business architecture first.' When I look at this reference paper, it makes me think of this as our business architecture, our business process."

Michelle looked delightfully flabbergasted. Seeing this as an opening to practice the Socratic method, she asked, "How do you think we apply this to our business architecture?"

"This DevOps automated governance will be our business process. We don't have to create anything. I'll take it one step further than just a baseline; let's start with this. Our goal can then be to move from left to right. Borrowing that Agile stuff you all talk about with iterations. Look at page fourteen," Andrea said, pausing.

Michelle took her tablet and switched from page eight to page fourteen on the big screen.

Andrea started back with, "Stage One, Source Code Repository. The risk says *Unapproved Changes* and the control says *Peer Review*. Isn't that the same thing as our first actionable item of *Enforce peer reviews of code that is pushed to a production environment*?"

"Yup," Omar replied. "If you look at page seventeen, it has things like unit testing, static security analysis, linting, and some other things I'm not familiar with . . . like immutable builds. Those look like a good start for one of those action items." Omar rustled through the papers in front of him and found the MRIA Outline printout.

"It's item two, *Identify and enforce minimum quality gates*," Omar read aloud.

Bill said, "Michelle, either our tail-chasing yesterday prepared us better for today's conversation, or Andrea, Omar, and Barry are better at getting to the point than we are."

Bill's attempt at flattery wasn't making Barry any more cheery. Bill continued. "We have a way forward for our first item, some ideas around the second item, so now we need to address the third: the developer access." He looked back down at this printout. "*Remove all elevated access to all production environments for everyone.*"

Bill didn't have to turn to Barry to signal for Barry to speak up. "Every new application has some type of break glass request that comes my way," Barry said. "We're always letting them into production machines, and most of these are not really break glass—they're not tracked and they are probably not revoked. I loved containers until the developers realized they could push into them. Omar, you should learn what 'immutable' means."

A mixed expression of embarrassment and interest came over Omar's face. He kept silent. Even though Barry's delivery was as rough as sandpaper, Omar knew all too well it was the truth.

Barry continued, obviously trying to be helpful so he didn't get an earful from Bill again. "If there is one thing this old man does, it's keep up to date with what's going on. I was at a DevOps Days event where someone was talking about tracking this. They had a metric for it; they called it 'Production Access Debt.' Every time a persistent production account is accessed, you add ten points. Each break glass read account is one point and each break glass write access is five points. The idea is to keep a zero value as an elite attribute. It's intended to drive the correct outcomes of automating and no human server access. This metric drives the correct outcomes, like more automation and less access to a server."

"That's very interesting," Bill said, encouragingly. "Can you tell us more about that?"

Barry got up from his seat and walked to the dry erase board. Grabbing a marker, he said, "Here's what I think we could do for this action item. Again, this is based on some things I've seen at recent conferences." He started making a list.

- Everything must be code.
- All logs must be streamed out.
- No system in production unless it has observability built in.

Looking at the board, Omar asked, "What do these mean? I mean, why?"

Barry smiled. "You know, I've been listening to you all. And I've seen what developers are doing around here. Everyone is cheering about automation, end-to-end

CI/CD pipeline, immutable infrastructure, SRE, observability, and all these shiny new things. But I want to ask our developers one simple question . . . if we really are that good at DevOps, automation, and infrastructure as code, why would anyone still need production access?"

Barry paused, looking for reactions. Omar was looking at the floor.

Michelle spoke up. "You're so right, Barry! I completely agree with you. I already discussed the 'everything must be code' concept with Tim and Jada, and they understand where we're going with this."

Barry grinned. "Really! I wasn't invited to that meeting. Guess I'm not that important."

"Oh, come on, Barry! You know it's not like that," Michelle said. "Tell me more about the other items on your list."

"Well, you want to remove *all elevated* access to production," Barry explained. "But taking it one step further, I think we should remove *all* access to production."

"Can we do that?" Michelle asked. "If we can, our auditors will love us! They probably won't believe us either, but that's another story. Right, Andrea?"

"I guess," Andrea laughed. "If you show me the list of the names of people with production access and the list is blank, I'll believe you!"

"To do this, as you all know, you need all code, including infrastructure code and of course the pipeline code, in source control," Barry continued.

"What's pipeline code?" Bill asked.

"It's the same idea as infrastructure as code. You do know what infrastructure as code is, right?"

"Yes, that's about the only thing in infrastructure I know about," he replied.

"I'll send you a link to a blog post from Capital One called 'Governance in a DevOps Environment.'[3] It it they wrote about taking concepts from infrastructure as code and applying it to CI/CD pipelines. The pipelines *themselves* are source controlled, just like the application code that passes through the pipeline. That way, changes to a pipeline are visible and provide a way to prevent unauthorized changes to how a pipeline operates. Not keeping an eye on the pipeline itself is how you find yourself in a situation similar to what happened to SolarWinds."[4]

"Tell me again why you want to remove all production access?" Omar asked.

Barry answered. "Because first, we want to make sure no one manually deploys code to production or makes any kind of changes there, and second . . ."

---

3. Jennifer Brady, "Governance in a DevOps Environment," Capital One blog (August 7, 2018), https://www.capitalone.com/tech/software-engineering/governance-in-a-devops-environment/.

4. SolarWinds was the subject of a major cyber attack that spread to the company's clients, affecting thousands of organizations around the globe.

Michelle jumped in with excitement, "And second, we all can encourage modern practices around logging and monitoring. In fact, with specialized log analysis and observability tools, we get a direct line of sight into the health of the system. We can even detect issues before they happen." Michelle paused to let that soak in before adding, "Our complex systems are noisy. Having a clear signal will reduce the cognitive load on our teams. Reducing that stress frees up capacity for higher value work. "

Barry added, "And that's exactly the reason why I have the other two points on my list."

There was silence in the room. Everyone thought this was a good idea, but it sounded too scary and involved too much work.

"So, as I was saying, if we do this, I can happily revoke all the developers' access. It will be a sweet win. I may even do it over a bottle of Scotch," Barry finally cracked a smile, surprising everyone.

Michelle found Barry's insights amazing. His previous life as an infrastructure admin was showing through.

The engineers on Omar's team had a ton of questions for Barry. Bill, Michelle, and Andrea sat by, listening intently. Both Bill and Michelle knew this type of open-ended conversation needed to happen. It's a common way to flesh out a design.

Bill looked up at the clock and realized they were nearly out of time. An hour had passed in a flash. He called the room to attention. "Hey, all." The room quieted down. "We need to wrap this up. Before we can move forward, I need a show of support for this proposed path. As I think Michelle has laid out, and this paper supports, automating governance is going to not only help us meet the concerns laid out in the MRIA but also, and maybe most importantly, prevent IUI from ever finding itself in this position again." Michelle nodded enthusiastically. "So, do we have the support of your respective departments to use this approach?"

Bill looked at Barry and Andrea.

"Obviously we'll have to take this up the chain," Barry said. Andrea nodded in agreement. "But it does look intriguing."

"Great. Okay, Michelle and I will formally document everything we did here today and send it out no later than tomorrow afternoon. We need you to take this back to your respective organizations and have conversations with your folks," Bill said, turning to Andrea and Barry.

"Let's get input and other insights as well. We're partially looking for any ways to make this better, but primarily we want to use this opportunity to start communicating our proposed changes. Letting everyone know where we're headed and where we may be headed is critical." Bill paused for a second in thought, then continued. "Let's take the next week to get feedback but also to experiment. We need to get to an implementation approach, but let's make sure we don't put the cart before the horse. Any questions?" Bill asked, taking another momentary pause.

Omar raised his hand, then started, "I have an idea for a tool."

Michelle quickly cut him off. "Omar, let's hold that for the next discussion. I'll set up a new chat room in the IUI messenger so we can have an open conversation. Put your idea for the tool in there."

Frustrated, Omar curtly replied, "Sure."

The meeting was over. Everyone started to gather their stuff and head for the door when there was a muffled ping. Those left in the room started patting their pockets for their phones.

Pulling his phone out, Bill saw a text message from his wife—a reminder to pick up a good Cabernet on his way home. She was cooking Wagyu for their dinner that evening.

"Do you feel confident you have enough for Susan's next huddle?" Michelle asked.

"Yes, yes I do," responded Bill, looking up from his phone at Michelle. "Listen, there's a BOGO sale at the supermarket and two bottles of wine with my name on them. Send me your notes so we can summarize all of this for the team, like we promised," Bill concluded as he rushed out the door with dinner on his mind.

CHAPTER 6

Tuesday, April 26th

Over the next several days, Bill and Michelle worked on a presentation outlining their proposal to move to an automated governance structure. They needed to get sign-off from Tim, Jada, and Jason before taking their proposal further up the chain to Susan and the board, and then submitting to the regulators. Michelle had already walked through some of the policy ideas at the initial findings meeting with Tim and Jada. They had been hesitant, so she hoped having Jason in the meeting with them would help smooth things over.

Luckily, since addressing the MRIA was top priority at IUI, they were able to get a meeting on the books quickly. Jason was excited by the idea and eager to see how it would be implemented, but others were hesitant.

"I don't know, Jason. Let's see what Laura and the outside audit team think before we sign off," Jada said.

"Yes, I want to think about this some more myself," Tim replied.

"We need to move on this quickly, so give me your final thoughts within the next two weeks. Then we'll fill Susan and the board in on our proposed direction. If they approve, we'll still need to formalize our proposed approach to the regulators and see if they approve it before our ninety-day deadline." Tim and Jada nodded, then Jason turned to Michelle.

"Once we have approval, you'll need to get started on an engineering solution. Pull together a team and let me know what you need to help pave the path forward."

Michelle nodded. "I have just the team in mind."

"Great work, everyone. I'm excited to see how that plays out, but remember, we're not even close to being finished here. I'm sure we can expect a long review process with the regulators while we deliver on our proposed promise. They're not going to just take our word for it, after all." Jason laughed. "Get ready for some good old-fashioned waterfall delivery dates and RAG status updates!"

"Oh, goody," Michelle replied with false enthusiasm.

RAG updates, those project templates with red, amber, or green stoplight icons indicating the state of the project, were a joke. They took hours of time to assemble but were full of subjective guesses and spin.

"I'm always ready for some good old watermelon reports," Michelle replied sarcastically.

"Watermelon reports?" asked Tim.

"Yeah, you know, waterfall delivery status updates that show green on the outside but are red on the inside," Michelle explained, causing even Jada to crack a smile. "I'll bring some crayons."

"That's the attitude!" Jason smiled and held his hand up in the air for a high five.

Michelle looked around and then, seeing that no one else was reaching forward, raised her hand toward Jason's. He slapped her hand with genuine enthusiasm before ushering them out the door. Not for the first time, Michelle was left wondering how Jason maintained his seemingly never-ending positivity.

Thursday, April 28th

Susan was staring out the window. The early morning sun was bright and painted the Charles River with a shimmering pool of light. She could hear Bill, Carol, Tim, Jada, and Jennifer talking behind her during their usual Thursday huddle. They were discussing the MRIA details and the automated governance response to the regulators that Bill and Michelle had put together.

"Excellent," Susan said as she turned around to face the team. "Are we ready to give this to the regulators?"

Jason jumped in. "It gets my vote! Not only should this satisfy the auditor, this automated governance proposal will better position us to maintain velocity on our digital efforts while respecting the guardrails."

"But I think there is still more to do," Jada said, adding caution. "Can the engineering team deliver or do we need to get them some help?"

Tim nodded in agreement.

Bill groaned. He had expected to hear another campaign to hire an external engineering consultant to fix all their problems. "I know it is going to be hard work, but I trust the team. We got this."

Jennifer nodded her head, as did Jason.

"I agree. I trust our team," Susan said, looking at the team then back out the window. "We'll update the board and the regulators on this automated governance plan. Bill, continue working with your team on the engineering solution and keep me informed on the progress."

Friday, April 29th

While the senior execs where working on passing their proposal through the approval process with Susan and the external audit firm, Michelle and her team, nicknamed "the Kraken," took over a section of "the dungeon" so they could all work together as they built out the automated governance solution.

There wasn't actually anything dungeony about the location. It was well lit and bright, but there were no windows to the outside world, hence the nickname. The teams had embraced the windowless cavern and themed the place as a medieval fantasy land. Cube walls were dressed to look like stone. The engineers were encouraged to make this space their own. Some decorated the walls and tables with dragons, swords, and jewels. It definitely added fun to the otherwise dull environment, and the team could use that about now.

Michelle had decided to hold a kick-off happy hour that afternoon as a way to build team unity. Even though this particular group had worked together before, Michelle thought it would be good to get everyone aligned to this special project. They were going to need to stay focused over the coming months if they were going to help get IUI through this storm.

"Great party, boss," Dillon, one of the site reliability engineers said, walking up to Michelle. "But maybe we shouldn't call it a happy hour anymore. I only see two people drinking anything alcoholic."

"You're right. But I think the name has stuck. Besides, you can attend happy hour without booze!"

"Hey, speaking of names, what are we going to name this project anyways?" Omar asked, and the whole group turned toward him, nodding their heads.

"I'm not sure any Greek names are available. It seems the Kubernetes community has commandeered every Greek word for their projects or products," Michelle said, laughing slightly. "What else could we do?"

"Whatever name we choose, make sure we can spell it easily," one of the other engineers said. "One of my friends launched an open-source project a few years ago from their company and no one could spell it right. It was a disaster."

With that, it seemed like every engineer pulled out their phone or tablet and started searching the web for Egyptian deities, Celtic gods and goddesses, and more. Nothing seemed quite right.

"I have an idea!" Omar interrupted. "Our source code repo generates random names. Let's pick the first name it generates." Everyone looked at each other. No one was in disagreement. Omar set aside his drink, pulled up a browser on his computer, and navigated to the source code repo. After a couple clicks and pounds, he said, in a horrible English accent, "I hereby pronounce thee 'Turbo Eureka.'"

"Turbo Eureka? That sounds like a vacuum cleaner," Dillon noted.

"I think it has an aura of cheeky prestige," one of the other staff engineers, responded.

"Turbo Eureka it is!" Michelle announced, lifting her glass of IPA into the air.

"Hear, hear," everyone cheered.

Michelle smiled. This was a great way to start. She just hoped they all kept up this level of enthusiasm for the project over the coming months. She had a feeling that this was going to be the most challenging project she'd ever worked on.

Michelle had spent almost all of her professional life in the finance industry, and she was all too familiar with how organizations dealt with regulations. She had experienced the same situation time and time again, where detailed system requirements became policy, and the policies kept growing and growing. At one point there were too many policies to keep track of, and people started ignoring them. No one cared. No one even knew where the actual policies were stored. Now it was just called bureaucracy and red tape.

As Michelle pulled her car out of the IUI parking lot later that evening, she reflected on how execution was tightly tied to the interpretation of these policies. It seemed as if the implementation begged the architecture, when in reality, the architecture of the system should drive the implementation specifics.

She seemed to experience post-traumatic stress when "the business" signed off on requirements. Without fail, there would be a need, not too long after the sign-off, to make a change. Some aspect of the system operations, development, process, or security would need to change. Michelle and her team had measured how much time it took to complete all the required paperwork for the change approval board. They were astonished when they calculated it to be just under five hundred person-hours.

Five hundred hours of pure work effort; not accounting for wait times when an email or feedback was holding up completing a change board requirement. The engineers constantly lamented how subjective the process was, joking that if they were to give the same software and policy to two different change approval board members, they'd get completely different answers.

Michelle merged onto the highway. As she drove down the congested road, the lanes of cars reminded her of IUI. Each lane reminded her of an organizational silo. These silos at IUI were being broken down by forced collaboration, visualizing work, and automation. Even with these advances, software delivery did not noticeably quicken.

She chuckled out loud as the person in front of her signaled they were going to merge into the lane to their right. Even though the car put on its signal and seemed to meet all the proper cooperative driving expectations, the merge itself slowed down traffic. Michelle started to think. *Even though we come up with processes and an enhanced understanding to speed things up, we never go any faster—we just create slowness elsewhere.*

Michelle realized that there was a fundamental flaw with the rigor of the change process. This rigor was not based on how the system needed to operate, it was based on what happened historically. The more severe the MRA, the more arduous and long-lasting the repercussions. It was as if no one cared what the underlying cause was; they just wanted to address the symptoms.

Addressing the symptoms as they exposed themselves was the catalyst for an ever-slowing software delivery process. It was always in the name of security and risk. More and more processes were created, more complexity was added to the systems, and more time-wasting meetings were required. It was like organizational scar tissue. It kept building up, slowing down the processes even more and frustrating everyone involved.

Many people attempted to standardize much of this overhead. They were never successful because of the differing ways the engineers operated and their inability to agree on a converged set of operation approaches. All of this resulted in an exponential increase in time and resources to build and operate their applications.

"Holy moly," Michelle shouted as she slammed on her brakes. A car ahead of her merged into her lane with no turn signal. As she started to pay more attention to the road, she saw it happen again and again. For a moment, it seemed as if the norm was for other cars to force their way into the spot they wanted to be in as opposed to using their turn signals.

This aggressive driving reminded her of policy exceptions. There were a lot of people who forced their way through the change board using policy exceptions. After all, policy dictated what was required for any change to occur. Either by sheer force of will or by someone with a larger political clout taking responsibility, teams veered in and out of production with policy exceptions.

Escalate everything! She remembered a lunch meeting where an IUI business leader bragged about how they were able to get so much done at IUI. "If someone or something is blocking you, don't stand for it: drive around, fight for it, escalate." She laughed to herself thinking about how Barry and Andrea would react to that.

As she turned off the freeway, she started thinking about the *DevOps Automated Governance Reference Architecture* paper. There was something about it that was brilliant, but she just couldn't put a finger on it.

As she pulled up to a stoplight, it hit her. "The DevOps automated governance takes subjectivity and makes it objective," she said as if she was talking to an invisible person in her passenger seat.

Michelle realized it wasn't necessarily the concept of a change board that was the issue; rather, it was the subjectivity of how the change process was managed that was the major contributing factor. Subjectivity was the reason two differing change board members could give a multitude of differing, and even conflicting, answers. The change process was not a process with a set of objective specifications. It was a process of people passing or failing software based on their own warm-and-fuzzies.

Maybe this was the reason for the lack of transparency, she thought to herself. You can only be transparent when you have something to point to. If you don't have an objective measure, you don't have anything to point to.

The organization depended upon the subjectivity of its people as opposed to objective measures. They were opinion-driven, not data-driven. "Am I the only one to think about this?" she said to that invisible passenger in the front seat.

Michelle had a breakthrough moment as she pulled into her driveway. *We trust our compliance outcomes to people who have the authority to make a decision. At best it is based on some policy and at worst it is subjectively based on anything else that could influence that person*, she contemplated as she unbuckled her seatbelt, grabbed her laptop bag and purse, and then opened her car door. *That's ridiculous*, she thought to herself. *No wonder it's so unclear, inefficient, and painful.*

Walking into the house, she continued to challenge her own thoughts. *If we can automate DevOps governance, what unexpected consequences could there be? Even if we are doing everything correctly, making clear and great documentation and abiding by policy, is there somewhere we could be misinterpreted?*

Michelle didn't want to be doing all the right things and still be viewed as violating policy. She knew the smallest infraction or policy violation would create even larger obstacles to broader adoption. Change at these financial institutions was a long process. The length of change multiplied, and further encumbrance by a mountain-out-of-a-molehill perspective of the slightest misinterpretation could render these new efforts moot.

In all these thoughts, Michelle realized she had only been thinking about the change board, Security, Compliance, and auditors. She hadn't fully considered the engineers themselves. The fastest way to upset an Engineering team is to undertake a more intense process to develop and deliver their software. She realized how essential it was to ensure that any automated change process was decoupled from the engineers.

This automated process must ensure that the existing feedback loops established are not altered in any negative way, she thought. As physicians say, "First, do no harm," she joked to herself. *And if this automated governance results in reduced friction for engineers, all the better!*

Michelle set her bags on the dining room table and walked over to the kitchen. She could hear her twins and wife laughing in the backyard. She walked to the back door and looked out on the twins running around. As she watched, she realized the kind of rock-and-hard-spot situation the team could end up in if they weren't careful to design the approach that considered all stakeholders in the IUI software development and delivery process.

Monday, May 2nd

Standing at the high-top tables in the Kraken's section of the dungeon, Michelle kicked off the first official meeting of project Turbo Eureka.

"Alright everyone," Michelle said, raising her voice high enough to ensure the whole team could hear. "We just received word that the execs presented our response to the MRIA to the regulators. But that was the easy part, if you can believe it. Now we need to fulfill our promise, and we have nine months to do it. We'll be having monthly demos and check-ins with the regulators, and we need to keep them up to date on our RAG status."

Michelle heard a few groans around the room. The Kraken team had been used to working in an Agile/DevOps manner for some time, being one of the first teams to migrate during the early days of IUI's transformation. Working in a waterfall manner with RAG status updates felt like a step backward.

"If we were to build a thing," Michelle said, looking around the room at her team, "a thing that would automate the whole process so that an audit like this MRIA would never happen again . . . how would we do it?"

Omar leaned in. "We'd start with the first control: peer reviews."

"Is that the easiest?" Michelle wondered.

"I don't know yet. But at least I know where to start. We already use Git[1] to automate a lot of our daily workflows. Adding another set of API calls won't take us long at all," responded Omar with an easy shrug. "I'll mock something up. Just give me a day."

"Okay, let's start there."

A few days later the team joined up again.

"Omar, let's see this prototype that you've been talking about all morning," Michelle said.

Omar stepped up to the board. "Okay, so check it out," he said as he gestured to his screen. "Um, can someone approve this pull request?" He forcefully clicked his mouse.

"Done," said one of the other engineers, giving a thumbs-up in Omar's direction.

---

1. Git is a tool used for software development with Git-based version control and includes or is bundled with CI/CD automation, as seen with tools like GitHub, GitLab, CircleCI, Jenkins, etc.

Omar moved his mouse toward the *Merge* button, which would join his changes with the main code base.

"Watch my console," he instructed as his eyes darted to the bottom left of the screen. In twelve-point mono spaced font, a green word was illuminated against the black background: PASS.

"See that there? There's the attestation. I even added color to the logging!" exclaimed Omar. "And see, it's in the database too." He tapped his keyboard once, revealing evidence of his claim in the console of his local database client.

"That's slick," Dillon said, nodding his head in approval. The rest of Team Kraken appeared equally impressed.

"Great work, Omar!" Michelle cheered. "That was quick. Walk the rest of us through how you achieved this." Michelle sat back and admired the way the team listened attentively to Omar's explanations.

The engineers in Team Kraken were known for their fast turnarounds. They typically worked in two-week sprints that ended every other Thursday with internal demos. These demos provided the team with an opportunity to show off their new features and receive feedback. Michelle loved these meetings because she and her team could see the reactions of their stakeholders when they finally had the chance to show off all of their hard work.

Michelle was invigorated by Omar's prototype. It wasn't much, but it provided a spark to a seasoned engineer who had grown accustomed to a mundane cadence of bug squashing and incremental feature enhancements. In Michelle's mind, this was an opportunity to engineer an entirely new set of capabilities that, if done right, would empower IUI engineers to operate at full speed with the confidence of knowing that they're in full compliance.

CHAPTER 7

Wednesday, May 18th

Over the next week, Team Kraken hacked away at Omar's prototype. They had all been so inspired by Omar's initial demo it seemed like everyone had ideas for features and capabilities.

During standup one morning, Omar asked the team, "What good is a record of pull request approvals if they can't be linked to a deployable version of the application?"

There was a brief moment of silence.

"I see where you're going," said Michelle, "but how do we connect a merged pull request to an artifact that hasn't been built yet?" She was referring to the continuous integration (CI) pipeline task of building and publishing an artifact to an internal registry. The CI pipeline ran after the pull request was merged, which meant that Omar's prototype attestation had no awareness of a deployable artifact.

"Hang on, I have an idea," muttered Omar. "Remember that pipeline plugin we built for last year's all-hands meeting—the one that forwarded build metadata to a database for reporting?"

Michelle nodded.

Omar continued. "Those payloads contain the artifact metadata and the commit URL. We can use the commit URL to associate the pull request activity to the published artifact."

"Yes!" Michelle said excitedly. "Let me add this to our backlog."

Wednesday, June 1st

After a more than a week of hacking, interrupted by a long Memorial-holiday weekend, the Kraken team finally circled up to prepare for the demo, but Omar had one more surprise for them. After his initial prototype, Michelle had challenged Omar to find a lightweight alternative to his colored logging—a more visually appealing way to display the PASS or FAIL status messages without the overhead of a web UI.

They had spun up this special task force quickly, pulling from an already established engineering team instead of creating a product team. This meant they had no UI dev onboard, and nobody on Team Kraken was up to date on the latest UI frameworks. Despite this, Michelle was confident her team would be able to pull something together that achieved their needs. Not for the first time, she thought about how IUI put together teams. She had recently read an interesting paper that was related to exactly this, arguing for full-stack teams instead of full-stack engineers, but that was for another time.[1] She'd have to remember to forward that paper around the office.

Michelle joined the prep meeting and immediately noticed the huge large grin across Omar's face. She figured he had an answer to her challenge.

"Omar, I'm guessing you have something for the team?"

"You're gonna love this," he said, commandeering control of the meeting screen. "You all know the drill by now; I need an approval on this pull request." After receiving the required approval, Omar merged and kicked off the pipeline. After the pipeline finished, Omar clicked over to the demo application's repository. "See the README?" he asked. Heads nodded around the room.

"Now, see that there?" Omar circled his mouse around the lower portion of his screen, which revealed three colored boxes: gray, blue and green. The green boxes provided the visual cue that the item had passed.

"That's so cool!" exclaimed Michelle. "How did you do that?"

Omar, with a sense of satisfaction from the team's approval, explained, "There's this open-source project called shields.io[2] that makes 'badges.' These badges can be placed anywhere that HTML renders, including README files. So I set them up to read our attestations and voilà! We've got a lightweight feedback loop for our demo."

1. Read more on the idea of moving from full-stack engineers to full-stack teams in the guidance paper *Full Stack Teams, Not Engineers* by Jason Cox, Christian Posta, Cornelia Davis, Dominica DeGrandis, Jim Stoneham, and Thomas A. Limoncelli at ITRevolution.com/resources.
2. Learn more about this open-source project at https://shields.io/.

"This is one of the coolest ideas I've ever seen," Michelle said. "It's right there in your repository too—the developers never need to look anywhere else!"

Omar's grin now stretched from ear to ear as he realized the added benefits of his clever idea.

The first prototype automated the attestation of approvers on a pull request to the primary branch of a repository and correlated it with an artifact build and version. It was a simple process that was initiated by a webhook configured in the application's source code management platform. A webhook is a common feature of most software that allows users to subscribe to events that occur on the platform. When one of these events occurs, it triggers a message to be sent to a given destination. Michelle had the system administrator of IUI's source code management platform configure a global webhook to send all metadata to project Turbo Eureka's receiver service whenever a pull request was merged.

The webhooks were reliable but didn't contain enough information about a pull request's activity. To help with that, the team engineered a "processor" that used the commit link in the webhook payload to execute an enrichment callback to the source code management platform. The callback gathered the history of activities on the merged pull request. After enriching the payload with pull request activities, the processor forwarded all the information to a service running a policy engine and used policy code to count the number of approvals from reviewers (other than the code authors) and provide a pass or fail ruling on the attestation. The pass/fail decision, along with the evidence, was then digitally signed (i.e., "notarized") and stored in the database.

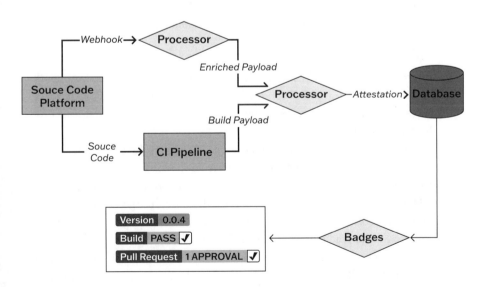

"This is great, team!" Michelle exclaimed, turning around. "I think we're ready for our first demo with stakeholders."

Thursday, June 2nd

"The purpose of this demo is to review the first actionable item," Michelle started. The first demo to the larger team, including stakeholders from Audit and Security, was finally here. Bill, Barry, and Andrea were all in attendance and eager to see what she and the engineering team had been working on for the past couple of weeks. If all went well, they'd be using this demo in their next check-in with the external audit team and regulators. She used her table to project the *MRIA Outline* document onto the screen in front of them.

Actionable Items

- Based upon the MRAs issued, the following items should be addressed
  with formal standardized approaches:
    - Goal: Define a minimally acceptable release approach
    - Objectives
      - Enforce peer reviews of code that is pushed to a production environment.
      - Identify and enforce minimum quality gates.
      - Remove all elevated access to all production environments for everyone.

"Enforce peer reviews of code that is pushed to a production environment," Michelle recited. "Our team has been working for the last month and a half, and I think we've made great progress." She turned to Omar. "Can you demo this feature in Turbo Eureka for us?"

"Yup, one sec. Let me take the screen from you," Omar replied. A moment later, Omar's screen appeared. All of his programs were dark, with differing bright colors for words. He had what seemed like hundreds of internet browser tabs open.

Andrea stared at the screen of code and laughed. "Is this the demo, all of this code?" Andrea inquired. "Because it all looks like Greek to me. I know it's code, but I have no idea how to read it or even start making heads or tails of it."

"No, sorry, let me navigate to our source code repo." After shuffling through his browser tabs as if it were an unorganized desk with papers all over it, the source code repo website came up. Omar maximized it on his screen so it was the only thing people saw.

"This was an easy one," Omar started. "Let's first talk about what we were trying to accomplish. We used page fourteen of the *DevOps Automated Governance Reference Architecture* paper as the basis for our approach. The risk we are addressing is *unapproved changes*, the control is peer review, the action that triggers the control to be enacted is a *pull request* merged into the main branch, and the actors are the *code author* and the *code reviewer*."

Michelle had a big smile. She was amazed that Omar, a software engineer, was using a language that a Risk person would. She asked herself, *Is this what they mean by shifting left with risk? Let risk management begin in the developer's mind?*

"Before I get hands on, let's talk about some things we learned," Omar said. "Our source control tool has the ability to require a reviewer for a pull request. But this wasn't enough, as Andrea and I discussed."

Bill nodded his head, excited to hear that the engineering team was already seeking out advice and input from Audit this early in the process.

"Audit needs a record that the pull request happened. So we needed to find a way to generate that record. This hasn't been done before. Other tools we use can issue a report, but the source control tool doesn't do that. Also, before I forget, we decided that we only need to do this for the main branch, no other branches. That's because code in the main branch goes into production. Other branches don't go into production, and some branches may never get merged into main."

Michelle interrupted. "Omar, before we go any further, can you explain to us all what pull requests, merges, branches, and the main branch are?"

"Are you freaking kidding me, Michelle, really?" Omar replied, in a half whisper, though everyone could hear him.

"We've failed in the past because the right people don't understand the process. And the right people include Barry and Andrea and especially their teams back in Security and Audit," Michelle said. "They need to understand how the sausage is made so they can help ensure we're including their concerns correctly."

Omar rolled his eyes as he accepted the task. "Okay, let me see if I can do this without explaining every aspect of source control and wasting everyone's time. The purpose of source control is to track changes to code. The main branch is the golden copy of your code. When someone needs to update the code, they make a copy and add their changes. This copy is called a branch.

"For example, when we branch from the main branch, we give our branch the name of the ticket number for the feature we're working on. So, let's say we have a new feature for ticket 112233. We'll create a branch with the name feature/112233. In branch feature/112233, we'll make all of our code changes.

"When we're done, we create a pull request. A pull request is pretty much as the name implies: it's a request to pull the changes from another branch—in our case branch feature/112233—into the main branch. When the pull request is created, that's when the code review happens. At that time, it's just a request; nothing's been merged into the main branch."

"What do you mean by merge?" Andrea asked, tentatively raising her hand.

Omar answered, "Merging is the process of taking the code changes from branch feature/112233 and incorporating them into the main branch."

"So merging is simply copying all the files from branch feature/112233 into the main branch?" Andrea responded.

"Um . . ." Omar turned to Michelle. "How technical do you want me to get here?"

"Just technical enough to help everyone understand."

"Okay, you can think of it as copying. But what merging does is literally merge the content from the two branches, so only the changes in branch feature/112233 appear in the trunk. In fact, the reviewer can see the exact lines or file, or parts of lines or files, that are to be changed in the context of the whole."

Andrea spoke up again, "Okay, let me restate to make sure I understand. When changes in some branch are ready to be brought into the main branch, and an engineer creates a pull request, this pull request kicks off a code review. That code review gives other developers an opportunity to see what is about to be changed and provide feedback on the changes. Then, I'm assuming when the code review is done, or done per the expectations of the review, the request is approved? And when approved, this is when the merge happens?"

"You got it!" Omar said.

Andrea replied, "I understand now. Tools aside, our auditing process is very similar. So, what we need is a) proof that a code review was made, b) who the code reviewers were, c) who the code authors were, and d) review activities such as any issues found in the review and evidence of those issues being closed or approved."

"I was just about to get to that," Omar said. "I have a demo source code repository here called Demo-Repo. There is one file called README.md. Inside this README file there is just one word, 'hello.' I want to change this, so I'm going to create a branch called *change-1.*" After some clicks and taps, a spot on the web browser changed from *branch: main* to *branch: change-1.*

Omar minimized the web browser and opened one of his coding tools. "Okay, I now have access to the new branch I created. I'm going to change the README," Omar said. He put his cursor after the word *hello* and added a space, then typed *world.* The text now read *hello world.*

After some more clicking and reopening the web browser with the source control tool, Omar continued, "Alright, I now have the changes ready for a pull request."

Omar hovered over a green button on the opposite side of the screen from *branch: change-1* that said *Pull Request*. He clicked the green button and a new screen popped up. It had many things on it, but one field of text was particularly important.

"Here is where I'll explain what my changes are and the reason for them." Omar typed *new requirement to add a subject of the hello*. After that, he moused to the bottom right of the screen and pressed a red button that said *Request*.

"Dillon, can you review and approve that pull request when I give you the go?" Omar said, looking across the room. Dillon turned around and gave Omar a thumbs up. They watched on Dillon's screen as he pulled up the pull request that highlighted the text *world* as the addition in *hello world* in the README.md file.

"Okay, we've simulated a change about to happen. When Dillon approves the pull request, the source control tool will merge it into main. Our continuous integration tool—we just call it the CI tool—will detect this merge and start doing other things. This part is where we spent a lot of time experimenting."

"So far, there isn't anything earth-shattering here," Barry said.

"No, you're right, but let me pull up the CI tool," Omar replied, shuffling again through the multitude of web browser tabs.

Another window appeared on the screen with what looked like a process flow at the top. Most of the bubbles were gray, but the very first one was blue. Inside the bubble, it said *Code Review Attestation*.

"Here, where it says *Code Review Attestation*. This is what we did. Let me explain what's happening under the hood. Sometimes these tech-demos suck, because the magic is happening behind the scenes," Omar said.

He continued, "We wrote a small program we call Code Review Reporter. The purpose of Code Review Reporter is to create something similar to a report and make sure that those things Andrea talked about happen. When the CI detects a change, the CI tool is given a critical piece of info, something called a *commit ID*. This commit ID is a unique identifier that identifies the merge and the pull request. What Code Review Reporter does is send the commit ID to the APIs of the source control tool and asks two things: the names of all the code reviewers and all code authors. When we get that data back, we create a file that lists the names of the reviewers and names of the authors, counts the reviewers' names, makes sure there is at least one reviewer other than the code authors, provides a number for the count of reviewers, and has a field we call *attestation*. In this field, if there is at least one reviewer that is not the author, we fill it in with *PASS*; if there's less than one, then it says *FAIL*."

Andrea, Bill, Barry, and Michelle looked super pleased.

"Okay, that's slick," Barry admitted.

Omar didn't know what to do with a positive comment from Barry. He smiled and felt a burst of energy hit him like a shot of espresso.

"That's not all," Omar said. "Now, if the attestation says *FAIL*, then the Code Review Reporter tells the CI tool to stop processing. Then, nothing else happens in the pipeline and the code cannot go to production. Heck, it can't even make it to its next steps. We call this *breaking the build*."

Everyone at the table was looking at each other. They were attempting to assess what the others thought of what Omar and the team had delivered.

"Something is missing here, but I can't put my finger on it," Andrea said.

Omar looked surprised. The excitement he had been enjoying suddenly died.

"What? What could be missing? I literally just accomplished building a tool to fulfill the first actionable item. Nothing can go to production without having at least one reviewer," Omar said with agitation, gesturing wildly at the screen as though no one had just seen the brilliance he had shown them.

"That is your segregation of duties right there. No single developer can make changes to code and send it to production without a second set of eyes reviewing it." Michelle looked at Andrea.

"Yes, on the surface this works, but something is missing. I just can't figure out what it is," Andrea replied.

Omar let out an exasperated sigh and crossed his arms.

Michelle said, "Andrea, let's set up some time to talk more about it. Could you take the rest of the day to compile your thoughts, and we can cover it on Monday?"

"Yes, I can do that," responded Andrea.

"Add me to that list as well," Barry requested.

CHAPTER 8

Monday, June 6th

That Monday meeting didn't happen.

Instead, Monday morning started with IUI's customer-facing website going down. Customers couldn't bank for nearly twelve hours. The Kraken team was pulled off Turbo Eureka and everyone was in firefighting mode, working well into the night trying to fix the problem.

Initially the blame was on IUI's cloud hosting vendor. But the issue turned out to be a gremlin in a "lift-and-shift-to-cloud" project named Omega that IUI had hired an outside firm to assist with and which was completed months ago. The project had seemed successful at the time, but now it looked like it had caused more problems than it solved. IUI didn't have the appetite to pull in enough funding to properly implement a cloud native solution. There was a push to "get on to cloud" by any means. At the time, the cloud infrastructure organization didn't care about how it was done; they only cared about the number of applications that were migrated onto the cloud. Every week they published a chart that showed the upward growth of cloud usage. Senior leadership had been very happy about the progress they made.

The senior manager responsible for project Omega had no prior experience in cloud technologies. On top of that, it was his first big project at IUI. He wanted to make a name for himself and told the external firm to do whatever they needed to do to get the application migrated to the cloud. Project Omega was seen to be a huge success, and the senior manager got promoted. But a small number of IUI engineers who were close to that project knew that the external firm cut corners and broke all kinds of cloud engineering principles. They had raised these issues with their management team, but their complaints were ignored. It was only a matter of time before a real disaster would strike.

While the team was able to restore some form of service within a day, it was quite clear that IUI needed to immediately assign their best engineers to fix the contributing factors to the failure. Michelle and Omar's team were pulled in to assist, along with many others. Michelle was worried they were going to fall behind on their delivery promises to the regulators.

Thursday, June 30th

Nearly a month into the incident, Michelle and her team found themselves at a town hall. Carol asked, "What could we have done better?"

Dillon spoke up. "For one, listen to us! We warned the team about this a long time ago. Every possible corner was cut to push this app into the cloud. Zero automation was put into place. They created layer after layer of single points of failure. Worse, without means for observability, there was no way for us to see problems. All of this piled up and grew even worse with each new upgrade. I guess you could say that technical debt finally broke the bank. But to be fair, we warned our management, and we know they warned leadership. This was avoidable, but clearly it wasn't a priority until now."

Gasps and muffled chuckles rippled through the crowd. Omar was doing his best to stifle his laughter. Michelle looked embarrassed not only for the Engineering teams but also on Dillon's behalf. Dillon's previous company had an open culture, where challenging things and speaking out directly was normal and welcomed. He was unaware of the mess he could be creating at this moment.

The town hall concluded quickly after Dillon's comment.

"You know how you know when a town hall is successful?" Barry asked, leaning over to Andrea and Michelle. "When everyone arrives happy and leaves pissed off."

Andrea pulled back from him and gave him a dirty look.

Walking down the hall and back to the dungeon, Michelle tapped Andrea on the shoulder. "Hey, how was it? You're not normally in these meetings," Michelle said.

"I had some time and decided to come and watch. Since I've been working so closely with your team, I admit I was curious. I feel bad for Carol; that had to be hard. Our town halls aren't nearly as exciting as yours are," Andrea replied.

"Not even when there are audit findings?" Michelle asked with a chuckle.

"No, nothing like that with audit findings," Andrea replied. "Listen, we never met up to talk about my thoughts regarding the last demo. Now that things seem to be simmering back down, do you have time?"

Michelle responded, "I sure do. I'm free this afternoon. Now that it appears this incident is over, I need the team to refocus on Turbo Eureka full time. We're about due for our next check-in with the external audit team and the regulators. Let's meet at the high-tops in the dungeon in thirty minutes."

Andrea and Barry were already in the dungeon when Michelle arrived. Barry was thumbing through a printout. A copy of the same printout was sitting in front of an empty spot at the table. Michelle assumed that was her spot.

Michelle picked it up. It wasn't too thick, about ten pages of front-to-back print. The cover said *Three Lines Model*.

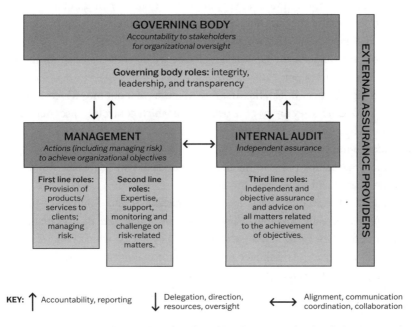

Source: "The IIA's Three Lines Model: An Update of the Three Lines of Defense," The Institute of Internal Auditors, last modified July, 2020, https://www.theiia.org/en/content/position-papers/2020/the-iias-three-lines-model-an-update-of-the-three-lines-of-defense/.

"Michelle, thanks again for meeting with me. I hope you don't mind, but I invited Barry as well. He and the Security team are key to this discussion," Andrea said.

"Is this specifically about security?" asked Michelle.

"No, it's about governance in general," replied Andrea.

"Okay, I'm confused, although I think you may be about to explain this to me," Michelle said with a smile as she took a seat.

"Yes, I am," Andrea replied. "The Three Lines Model, formerly called the Three Lines of Defense, is a model for governance in highly regulated organizations like ours. It was created by the IIA, the Institute of Internal Auditors. In essence, governance is simply the process of identifying and making promises, and then checking that you keep those promises. The Three Lines Model attempts to bring structure to this concept. I was a bit concerned about Omar's demo back before this Omega fiasco. What I saw there was a good start, but it didn't seem to include aspects of the Three Lines Model, which we use at IUI to control risk. It goes beyond IT."

"How do we currently do this in other areas? And what do the three lines look like when done *properly*?" Barry asked.

"Let's start with our bank tellers," Andrea said. "Bank tellers are the first line. The bank tellers at our organization own and manage the reduction of risk associated with their responsibilities. It's very important to have their input into designing the controls because they are the people who execute the control procedures on a daily basis—they know which ones work and which ones don't."

"Are you telling me the bank tellers decide which controls to apply and which not to?" Barry blurted out.

"Well, in a perfect world, the first line would have input into which controls do and don't work, but they are not the deciders of which controls to use. Actually, and unfortunately, most of the time they don't get asked for input. The second line just railroads them," Andrea responded.

"Audit railroading the working person. Sounds like we share a common understanding," Barry said with some sarcasm.

"Actually, the second line is the risk management and compliance functions. Their purpose is really threefold. They decide how to structure the risk management framework for their respective organizations. They decide which policies and controls to put into place. And they're responsible for making sure that the first line is executing within the established controls and policies."

"So what does the third line do? It sounds like the first two do everything," Michelle said.

"The third line is an assurance mechanism. They don't decide what controls to use or how to implement them. They're responsible for assessing if the risk management approach put in place by the second line is effective. The third line's primary responsibility is to ensure that there are clear promises being made, that the promises are being kept, and that the whole promise approach is effective for the organization. These folks generally provide their findings to higher-level company executives and sometimes the board of directors," Andrea said.

"Does this even apply to IT?" Barry asked.

"Here's my recommendation, and tell me if this doesn't make sense. Your first line is your engineers. They have the most context of your software, and they should be implementing the control procedures. The second line is Security. Barry, you should be working with the engineers to define and select the controls. The third line is Audit. If done well, it can be as independent as possible as a third party to see how someone like you, and say, Omar, establish a risk management approach and operationalize it."

Andrea could see the wheels turning in both Barry and Michelle's heads. They were thinking hard.

"What you just said isn't really anything new," Barry responded. "But—and this is a *big* but—how you laid out the roles and responsibilities of the three lines . . . well, I can appreciate that explanation. Most of our knucklehead engineers think I'm shoving security requirements down their throat. And most of the time, I am. But it's because there's no other choice. Ignorance pervades those keyboard monkeys." Barry paused for a second to gather his thoughts. His eyes brightened as if an idea just came to him.

"Don't let anyone know I said this," Barry continued, "but the three lines perspective could make my job easier. Most of the time, I not only tell the engineers what controls to abide by, I also have to figure out how to implement them. With the three lines model, it would be up to the first line to figure out how to design and implement the controls. All I need to do is validate that their implementation is proper."

"Can that actually work?" Michelle asked. "I mean, it sounds great in theory, but can it really work? Do we have the culture for it?"

Barry quickly responded with a full belly laugh. "No, not this culture. Although this culture is the culture that got us into this mess. So, evidently something needs to change."

"I agree with you, Barry," Andrea said. "Michelle, that's why I wanted to talk with you. When I saw what Omar was doing, it was great, but it condensed all three lines into one. What he showed was as if the engineers determined everything. We need a way to ensure there are at least two lines."

"Do you have any idea how we do that?" Michelle asked, looking at both Barry and Andrea. The pause felt like a lifetime. By now, each of them needed a brain break. There was significant contemplation going on and a great deal of angst to accompany it. Ideas were bounced around, but they kept wracking their brains on the *what ifs*. They were on the verge of damning an idea by what if-ing it to death before even trying it out.

Michelle started again, but this time she started drawing out a diagram. "So . . . let's go back to first principles: What are the fundamental concepts? What do we need? First, we need a control. For example, *peer review*. Right?" She continued without waiting for an answer. "Second, we need a policy. Something that says *a peer review must be done by one person other than the code author*. There could be a legitimate case where more than one person needs to review a change. Which means we want to treat this policy as a configuration so that we can change it when we need to. Third, we need a way to collect *evidence* that a peer review was done. Fourth, we need to validate the evidence against the policy—in an automated way."

"Isn't Omar already doing this?" Barry asked, staring at the diagram Michelle was drawing. "I can't believe I'm defending him right now, but his demo did all those things."

"It did, but there's a problem. He has a policy hard-coded in his tool. The second line, for example, should be able to change parameters of that policy in a way that doesn't require the tool to be updated or rewritten," Michelle responded.

"That makes sense. It's the knucklehead knob. Externalizing the policy, like you're talking about, allows us to turn things up or down while at the same time making sure these don't cause any adverse effect on the developers. Is this the type of separation between line one and two you were referring to?" Barry asked.

"I think so. Some of what you and Michelle just said went a little over my head, but I think we're on the right track. Can we prototype something like this?"

"The team would love nothing more than to get their hands dirty again with real, interesting work, not this ridiculous shift-and-lift remediation work. Barry, set up some time with Bill and Omar. Bill should be there so he can help prioritize features for this. And so he can understand the customer value. We can then rehash this conversation with Omar. I think we set them up with another spike and time box for two weeks. Based on the way they work, they'll have something that meets our needs, although it may not be pretty. But we can worry about that later."

Thursday, August 4th

Five weeks had passed since Andrea, Barry, and Michelle had discussed getting a new prototype built. The concept was simple enough, but some of the details were just out of reach or would require a bit more work.

Omar was always telling Bill and Michelle that he'd have a demo tomorrow. He did this every day the first week. Bill had nicknamed him the "little technical wolf" and joked that Omar would "huff and puff and tell you it's easy, and then have more excuses than results tomorrow."

Tension from the leadership team was also getting palpable. Susan had barely sat down for the latest huddle before ammunition began firing.

"It's been nearly five months since we first got hit with the MRIA, and over two months since we began our execution plan. And there is barely anything to show," Jada said in a loud, almost demeaning voice. "We need to show the regulators and external audit team that we're making more progress."

Tim joined her. "Barry filled me in on the lack of progress. I'm beginning to question if the engineering talent we have internally can pull this off. Carol, have you considered hiring an outside firm to engineer this for us?"

Carol was flabbergasted. *Have they not realized we just spent a month cleaning up a disaster that project Omega left for us?* she screamed in her head.

"No, there's no need to assess another firm to do this for us," Carol said. "There was a significant delay with the large system outage, as you all know. Tim, I believe it was a senior manager of yours who was responsible for that project."

Carol paused for a moment and looked piercingly at Tim. Tim had a scowl on his face but didn't immediately say anything. Carol suspected that having Susan in the room was keeping him from saying exactly what he thought.

"While I'm not intending to point fingers, when we fail, we fail as a team," Carol said. "Unless you want me to make this about your organization's capabilities?"

Feeling the tension, Bill said, "The team we have right now is the team responsible for some of our best products. We can pretend this is like everything else, or we can be realistic. This is an investment in continuous improvement. How do we prefer to couch it as leaders?"

"Team Kraken has done something that had never been done before: they were able to automatically perform policy audits on their own internal software as it went through the build and deploy processes. Andrea and Michelle also spent a significant amount of time educating the engineering team on the IIA's Three Lines Model. Collectively, they figured out how to reallocate human auditors from doing time-consuming and error-prone manual audits and instead focus on designing better controls and enhancing the IUI risk framework. Tim and Barry also started discussing ways to automate security controls," Bill finished.

"I understand and can appreciate the progress," Tim conceded. "But time isn't on our side. We need to do whatever we can to get this done."

Susan nodded her agreement. "Tim is right. The runway is running out. I know the team is working hard, but the massive site outage we just experienced has our board members even more on edge. We can't afford to miss our deadlines with the regulators or it's game over. This is our top priority. Let me know if you need any resources whatsoever."

Susan paused to survey the room and then added, "You have a blank check. I expect you to use it if you need it." Susan stood up to leave.

The gravity of the situation hit everyone in the room and they all nodded in agreement, looked at each other, and stood to leave as well.

"Thank you, Susan," Bill said and then looked at everyone standing and added, "Carol and I are headed down to check in on the team. You are all welcome to join us." Jason enthusiastically agreed. Bill, Carol, and Jason left the huddle and headed to the elevator.

"You'll have to tell me more about project Omega sometime," Jason said as they entered the elevator.

Carol gave a small chuckle, and Bill shook his head. "That's definitely a two-finger Scotch conversation."

Jason laughed as the doors started to close.

"Dammit! You can't be serious! . . ." was heard along with a string of other expletives as the elevator doors to the dungeon opened. Michelle, Bill, and Jason stepped off, awkwardly looking at each other like they had been dropped into a demilitarized zone. It seemed like the team was currently taking on heavy fire. "NO!" came another loud scream from across the room.

"Michelle, are we sure about not hiring an outside engineering firm?" Bill joked, trying to manage a smile.

"Bill, don't test me," replied Michelle.

They all rounded the hallway corner to see the engineers, Barry, and Andrea standing around Omar's desk looking stressed and perplexed.

"What's the problem?" Michelle asked as she approached the crowd.

"I'm not sure what's happening. It's not working," Omar finally replied, nearly choking on each of his words. Omar spun around in his chair to look at Michelle. He quickly composed himself as he saw that Jason has joined the group. "We . . . well . . . we were looking good just a couple days ago. And the team thought we could add some of our other control gates to the automated governance approach in time for the next big demo."

"No, not 'we.' You—*you* thought we could add other control gates," Dillon interjected, staring intently at Omar. Omar shot Dillon a stern look, obviously upset.

"Let's start from the beginning. Walk us through it all," Michelle said, calming the situation down.

"I can't. It doesn't work. I need to figure this out first," Omar replied.

"Omar, take a deep breath, step back, and let's review it," Michelle said.

"Yeah, review it, like with other people and get their input," Dillon added.

"Okay, everyone. Let's huddle up over there at the high-tops and work this problem together," Michelle said. "Omar, bring your laptop over."

Omar reluctantly gave in. He gathered his things from his desk, and they all moved to the high-tops on the floor. It was crowded—very crowded. From an outsider's perspective, it might have appeared as if there was a sneak preview for a movie going on. There were even folks bringing over candy and drinks from the snack bar nearby.

"Dude, mouth closed!" Omar sniped at one engineer munching on a candy bar. "Okay," he continued, taking a breath and trying to calm down after Michelle shot him a warning look. The usual collection of web browser tabs appeared on his screen. "We . . ." Omar started to say, but Michelle cut him off.

"Omar, before you start going through your code, walk us through the design," Michelle said.

"Design?" Omar responded with a confused look.

"Yes, the design of the system. The components, how they fit together, and the interfaces," Michelle responded.

Barry started to chuckle and said with a smirk, "Does your design include duct tape and bubble gum?"

Omar's face started to flush red.

"Omar, deep breath, seriously. It looks like you aren't breathing," Michelle said.

Omar sat back down, took his deep breath as instructed, and then looked back at Michelle.

"Remember the last demo, that report we created?" Omar asked.

"Yes," responded Michelle.

"We took that file and used our policy engine to analyze it," Omar said.

"What's a policy engine?" Andrea asked.

"It evaluates our attestation against a policy," Omar said. He continued on with the explanation. "Think of the attestation as a form, a form that is filled with information. For example, let's talk about the code review attestation. The attestation has two fields: a field to list all the reviewers' names who were not code authors and a field that has the count of reviewers. Let's call these fields *reviews* and *reviewers-count*. Then there's another form, the policy. Each attestation has a policy, so for the code review attestation, there's a code review policy. In that code review policy, there's a line that says *reviewers-count >= 1.*"

Andrea spoke up, "Omar, does that mean there must be at least one reviewer?"

"Yup," Omar replied. "You got it."

"As another example," Omar continued, "here's an attestation with two reviewers, so the *reviewers-count* field equals two. Now it compares the numbers. Given two is greater than or equal to one, the policy engine returns a report that says the code review passed."

"The term *policy engine* made me feel like this was more complicated than you just described," Andrea said.

"It gets more complicated, but that's the basics of how it works. We've been experimenting with a better way to assess code reviews for our Git repo—sorry, that's a Git 'repository' for the non-developers . . ."

Andrea gave him a thankful nod.

" . . . with different types of policy engines. We played with OSCAP and OPA . . . uh, OSCAP stands for Open Security Content Automation Protocol. It uses a language called SCAP, or Security Content Automation Protocol, to define security controls and automatically assess and audit them," Omar clarified, receiving a grateful grin from Andrea. "OSCAP is used in many places for assessing infrastructure compliance. I learned this while watching many online videos," Omar said with a grin.

Michelle nodded and encouraged him to continue.

"There's also OPA, or the Open Policy Agent. OPA is similar to OSCAP, except OPA is easier to use, or at least we think so. In OPA, you can write your policies in a language called REGO. We don't know who is going to be writing policies for this yet, but REGO is a lot easier to use than SCAP. If we have to write the policies, we'd rather use REGO.

"Here's a sample control we were playing with. We think it may be a better way to analyze code reviews than the way we do it now," Omar said, pulling up one of his tools.

"I agree," Andrea responded. "I want to use this as a prime example of how first- and second-line functions can collaborate in IT."

"Omar," Michelle called out, looking up from her own laptop. "I think I know your bug issue. Your JSON attestation file . . . is the object supposed to be named *action* or *actions* with an *s*?" she asked.

"It's supposed to be . . ." Omar said, trailing off and looking sheepish. "You've got to be kidding me. It's supposed to be with an *s*. Well, I guess this is a great example of the value of peer review."

Highly embarrassed, Omar flicked through his screens, changing text in differing files. No more than two minutes later, Omar turned to Dillon and asked in a much softer voice, "Hey, man, can you approve the test pull request?"

With the click of a button, the web browser displaying the continuous integration tool interface came to life. The first blue bubble, which said *Code Review Attestation*, turned green. Then the bubble after that, which was gray, turned blue. Only a few seconds later, it turned green. This happened for the next four bubbles.

"That's freaking embarrassing," Omar said. "Sorry about that, everyone."

"We've all been there, Omar. Sometimes we just need to slow down and take a breath, get some fresh eyes on something," Michelle said.

Barry spoke up with uncharacteristic enthusiasm in his voice. "You know what we did today?" Looking around, no one said a thing. "We applied the same concepts of infrastructure as code to our governance. I'm going to go out on a limb with this one. Omar, what you showed with REGO, you showed policy as code. Our policies can be source controlled, just like our software and some of our infrastructure."

"Policy as code?" Andrea asked, with a confused expression. "Does this mean that Audit and Risk need to hire developers and learn to write code? Your demo seemed great, but if we have to write code, I'm not sure this will work."

"Um, I guess we didn't think about that," Omar said.

Michelle responded, "No, I don't think so, Andrea. This is where we can collaborate. Based on how things are being built, someone will need to understand how to write the policies into the REGO, but it doesn't have to be Risk. We can have a policy team. Andrea, or Barry, when we need to implement a control with this approach, an engineer can be there to help. They can write this policy file on your behalf. We can limit the people who can push to the policy-as-code repo, and we can even make you, or whoever is the right person in Risk, the approver for pull requests into that repo."

"Is this how the new system will operate in the long term?" asked Andrea.

"I don't know. What we could do is look at the next iteration. Possibly some type of user interface for the compliance groups?" Michelle said aloud.

Andrea had a hesitant look on her face.

"Andrea, I understand your concern," Bill offered. "Michelle makes a good point. Jason and Michelle, for our next huddle with Susan, let's bring this up. We may need a small team in the short term to help out with this. Let me be clear, I don't want to throw the baby out with the bathwater. What we saw here today was great. But I'm under no impression this is the end all be all, although we are delivering what we set out to deliver. I'll volunteer to help you with the internal issues. After all, this is a product, right? So it will need a product team."

Clapping started to fill the room and everyone started looking around. It was Jason.

"Well done, Team Kraken!" Jason said. "Bill is right. There is more to do. But I don't want us to miss this golden moment. We just leveled up! And, Omar, great demo."

Omar blushed a bit. The rest of the team smiled and joined in on the applause. It had been a difficult past few weeks, and it was really nice to hear some appreciation from IUI leadership.

It was clear from the faces in the room that the team felt a new surge of energy. They could do this!

CHAPTER 9

Thursday, September 1st

The next month flew by quickly. With the post-lift-and-shift Omega project in the rear view mirror and a renewed energy from their recent successes, Team Kraken was making significant progress with Turbo Eureka. The turbo of Turbo Eureka was really working! They had implemented more quality gates and really felt like they were on a roll.

Michelle and Bill had just finished giving another demo session to a broader audience. Other people within IUI were becoming interested in what the team was doing. They were even using Turbo Eureka to automate the governance for all Turbo Eureka software they developed.

Michelle sat down at her desk and looked at her calendar. It had now been six months since they had first received the MRIA. She opened her laptop and navigated to the MRIA Outline document in the MRIA Madness folder. She had been keeping track at a high level of Team Kraken's accomplishments.

Actionable Items

- Based upon the MRAs issued, the following items should be addressed
  with formal standardized approaches:
    - Goal: Define a minimally acceptable release approach
    - Objectives
      - DONE: Enforce peer reviews of code that is pushed to a production
        environment.
      - Identify and enforce minimum quality gates.
        - DONE - Unit Tests
        - DONE - Source Code Quality Analysis
        - DONE - Static Application Security Test
        - In Progress - Software Composition Analysis
    - Backlogged Remove all elevated access to all production environ-
      ments for everyone.

The team had even been able to add some nice features to the Git repo. They continued using the open-source project that created software for badges that were color coded to make it easy to visually understand the status and quality of the software in a Git repo.

Michelle pulled up Team Kraken's Git repo on her computer. In the middle of the screen, offset to the left a bit, she saw the badges.

This repo had a badge with the status of every quality gate, showing whether the most recent quality gate passed or failed. The first badge simply showed the version of the software. The left part of the badge had a gray background with white writing that read *Version*. The right-hand side of the badge had a baby blue background color with gray text that said *0.0.4*.

Demo App

Version 0.0.4
Unit Test PASS ✓
Build PASS ✓
Code Review PASS ✓
Branching PASS ✓
SCA FAIL X

Below the version badge, there was a badge that read *Unit Test*. The right-hand side of the badge had a green background with the word *PASS* in it followed by a check mark. There were a few more subsequent badges that showed green, just like the unit test badge. Then there was one that read *Software Composition Analysis*. The right-hand side of the badge was red with the word *FAILED* inside of it and a large X.

"Omar, have a second?" Michelle hollered across the floor.

Omar got up from his desk and walked over to Michelle, looking at her screen. "What's up?"

"Why is the software composition failing for this repo?"

"Let's see . . . what's the latest commit number for main?"

Michelle clicked around on the web browser and highlighted some text. "The most recent commit to main is *9349c9b*."

"Okay, hold on to that number. Open another browser tab and go to https://attestations.investmentsunlimitedbank.com."

Michelle typed the address in.

"Okay, paste the commit number into that box," Omar said, pointing to a box labeled *Enter Commit Number* on her screen.

Michelle pasted the number into the box and clicked *Find Attestation*. A table popped up. It only had one row. She clicked *View Attestation* and the page refreshed, rendering all of the different attestation files. She scrolled down until she saw a title with *Software Composition Analysis* inside of it.

There was a lot of information in this part of the file. She saw recognizable sections that were named *High*, *Medium*, and *Low*.

Omar pointed at these sections. "Those are lists of common vulnerabilities and exposures—CVE for short. See, right there," Omar said as he read the screen. "Look at this *Critical*: CVE-2021-44229. If you remember, by policy, there shouldn't be any CVEs in the critical or high category."

"Do you know what that CVE is for?" Michelle asked.

"No, we'd have to look it up. But on the bright side, it looks like Turbo Eureka is working!"

"I guess it is," Michelle replied. "Okay, thanks for the info."

Omar turned around and went back to his desk.

Michelle scrolled through the attestations website a bit longer. She was impressed with all the information they were collecting and the controls they were implementing.

A few hours later, Omar came up to Michelle. "I just saw in my Twitter feed that there's a new Java vulnerability causing problems. Do you remember which CVE you saw this morning?"

"Who's they?" Michelle asked.

"Look at this. It looks like some security firm," Omar replied, showing her his phone. "But it's really started to blow up on Twitter. Can you pull up the one that you asked me about this morning?"

"Yeah, one sec." Michelle spun around to her laptop and pulled up the attestations website again.

"Oh, yeah! It's the same one!" Michelle practically shouted.

"Have you heard anything from Barry?" Omar asked.

"Not a thing. Let me reach out and find out?" Michelle picked up her phone and started typing.

Hey Barry, have you heard anything about this new critical CVE thing? Some Java vulnerability that's blowing up on Twitter?

Omar went back to his desk.

Michelle waited for Barry's response for some time, but eventually evening rolled around and she headed home. Maybe she'd find Barry tomorrow and ask him about it.

"Mmm. I think the fruity flakes are my favorite," Michelle said.

"No way, Mom. The peanut butter and chocolate puffs has that beat any day." One of Michelle's sons was spooning ice cream into his mouth as fast as he could.

"I'd have to agree," her wife said.

Michelle was with her twins and wife at Revolution Ice Cream. Her twins had melted ice cream running down their faces. She couldn't help but notice most of it was on their shirts.

Michelle's phone pinged and vibrated. "Nope," she said while fishing for her phone. "Fruity flakes all the way." She found her phone at the bottom of her purse and looked at the text.

Michelle, can you call me? it read. It was from Barry. It wasn't common for him to text Michelle, especially after hours. Barry was an email person. He hadn't even warmed up to chat. She got a bit tense.

Out with the family. Wait until tomorrow? Michelle texted back. She knew what the answer would be, but this was her polite way of telling people to bug off.

Me too. This can't wait, Barry's short reply said.

"Oh no, not another one," Michelle muttered. She started to get nightmares from the lift-and-shift Omega fiasco not so long ago. Was that acting up again? She and the team had done a significant refactor to the application. Then she remembered the CVE she had asked Barry about earlier that day.

Her wife looked over. "Everything okay?"

"Can you watch the kids for a second? I need to make a call. Something's up at work, and I need to check in on it."

"Sure."

"Thanks," Michelle said as she scooted out the door.

"Michelle, we're up shit creek without a paddle," Barry said when he answered Michelle's call. "Our Network Operations Center picked up some suspicious network traffic earlier today. Lucy called me a little earlier saying she got a text from the NOC to join a call. And I'm just now seeing your text. What's going on? I'm worried it's related to the chatter we're hearing too."

Michelle replied, "I was thinking of asking you that. You're the security guy. All I know is . . ."

Barry didn't let her finish her sentence. "Michelle, I'll have to call you back. We may have a problem here. Tim is pinging me. Bye."

Michelle's heart sunk deep into her stomach, so much so that her ice cream almost made an encore.

Michelle scooted back inside. "Grab some to-go lids for the kids. We need to cut this short," she said to her wife. She stood up and reached for the twins' ice cream cups. "Can you drive? I may need to take a few calls on the way," Michelle added.

Five minutes later, Michelle's phone rang. It was Barry again.

"What's up?" she asked.

"It's bad. That network chatter is related to the critical CVE that you texted me about. Tim said the NOC is getting flooded with alerts. I have friends texted me from other companies. I'm about to hop on a call with our security consultants at AlertFirst see what they know." Barry paused.

"What do you want me to do?" Michelle asked, hoping she wouldn't have to get on her laptop tonight.

"Stand by? After this call with our friends at AlertFirst I'll know more," Barry said.

Over the next hour, Barry kept Michelle up to speed via a flurry of texts on their inter-office communication channel. According to AlertFirst, a security consultancy IUI hired for computer forensics and penetration testing among other things, what was happening at IUI was not an isolated incident. In fact, it was quickly turning into a global firestorm.

Soon, news of the vulnerability was everywhere, even trending on social media. Companies around the world were scrambling. Technology teams from every sector were all focused on this one issue. It was as if someone had hit an international "pause" button on everything else in the tech space.

As the night rolled on, it turned out the vulnerability was pervasive yet overwhelmingly elusive. Every time the IUI NOC team thought they had addressed every vulnerable application, a new one would surface or a third-party software would publish a new patch. All other work at IUI was suspended while they directed their efforts to eradicating the vulnerability.

Friday, September 2nd

"Michelle, I think our security consultants found something interesting," Lucy said. Lucy was on IUI's security team and was an expert on IUI's central logging platform, which was used to collect any data that was created by applications and hardware under IUIs control.

She was grinning from ear to ear. It was clear that Lucy was enjoying the challenge, unlike everyone else in the NOC and most of IUI's technology team, who looked like they had just survived an harried expedition across a dense, dangerous jungle.

"What's up," Michelle asked, worried it was going to be more bad news.

"I was on the phone until late last night with our AlertFirst consultants," Lucy answered, looked excited rather than bothered. "The NOC has kinda stopped the bleeding for now, but the patient's still in serious condition. This is a critical vulnerability, as you know, and we still haven't fixed it or found a cure yet. No one has. We're all just on damage control."

Lucy continued, "Anyways, what I wanted to talk to you about is this, it seems this vulnerability is being caused by a specific Java library. Our AlertFirst consultants believe this as well, and we're hoping you can help us confirm. Can you help us check our applications for this dependency? "

As Lucy was trying to pull up her notes from last night, Barry and Andrea came walking over to listen in on Lucy and Michelle's conversation. Everyone at IUI was deeply involved in the incident. With the MRIA still over their heads, they couldn't risk a breach.

Michelle replied, "Hmm, that's a pretty common dependency. I wish I had better news, Lucy, but it might take some time to find them all. Omar, can you cross-check our applications for this dependency?"

Omar began pulling up Git repositories and everyone stood around awkwardly, wishing they had some way to help. But this was just going to take time.

"So, while we wait, I'd love to understand this better. What is a 'dependency?'" Andrea asked.

Michelle turned to Andrea, "It's an open-source library that we use in our applications."

"An open-source library?"

"Oh, well, software engineering, at its heart, is simply writing code. Like instructions to bake a cake—well, a highly complex cake," Michelle said, tapping her foot impatiently on the floor while staring over Omar's shoulder.

"But there are lots of ways to bake a cake, and there are lots of steps," she continued. Andrea listened intently. "While we may write a lot of code ourselves, kind of like writing our own recipes, we save a lot of time and effort just grabbing bits from others. You know, why reinvent the wheel when the code is already out there in the open? You can use this 'open' software that is stored in public code repositories or you can use bundles of this software that we call 'libraries.' Our code depends on these libraries. These are our applications' dependencies."

"Oh, so you're using pieces of someone else's recipe to bake your own cake?"

"Yep," Michelle replied.

Everyone continued to watch as Omar went through Git repositories on his laptop. Every time he found an app using the dependency, he put a check mark by the app's name on a sheet of paper, a list that was quickly growing longer and longer.

Michelle asked, "Omar, can't you look at just the Java repositories?"

"Wish I could tell just by their names," Omar replied.

"So, when you open a repository and find it's using Java, can you tell if it is using the dependency?" Michelle asked again.

"I think I can tell if our code is directly using this dependency. But I couldn't tell easily if it's a transitive dependency," Omar replied.

"Transitive dependency?" Andrea asked.

"Basically it's like the recipe we borrowed had already borrowed a recipe, or bits of the recipe, from someone else," Michelle said, a little frustrated.

Andrea gave her a quizzical look.

"Let's say we want vanilla icing for our cake, but we don't want to make it from scratch. So we get the premade stuff from the store. But the company that made that icing didn't want to make their own vanilla flavoring from scratch; they bought it from somewhere else. That's a transitive dependency."

"So if the vanilla used in the icing is bad, my cake will be bad, and I have no control over it?" Andrea asked.

Lucy burst out, "Yup. It's a software supply chain problem. Just like if your icing company bought vanilla flavoring that had been tainted or whatever." Lucy looked like she was going to explode with excitement. She was the only one. Everyone else looked like they could use about a week's worth of vacation time on a secluded beach.

"You see, a supply chain is the entire production flow. It's everything involved to deliver a product: the people, the materials, and the activities that produce a product like a vanilla frosted cake. The only difference here is that we're not talking about a cake, we're talking about software."

Andrea got excited for a minute. "This is fascinating."

"Really?" Omar quipped.

Lucy continued, ignoring Omar and engaging directly with Andrea. "The problem is, when I go to a store to buy a cake or vanilla frosting, I'm not likely to ask who produced the vanilla flavoring. And it might not even be something the frosting company or grocery store readily knows!"

"No," responded Bill, "I wouldn't even think to ask. I trust the store I'm buying from, therefore I trust they wouldn't purchase any bad vanilla or software with bad dependencies."

"That's a good point," Lucy said. "Because you trust the store, you're implicitly trusting the full supply chain of the cake. You're trusting all the people, activities, and resources involved in that supply chain. "

"We probably do the same thing in software. If we trust the software vendor, we trust the whole supply chain of the software," Bill commented.

"I may be changing the topic a bit," Andrea joined back in the discussion. "But I find developers trust open-source software more than vendor software."

"Isn't that natural? I mean, everyone can see the code!" Omar added, still slowly adding apps to his list.

Lucy responded with a question: "Are you sure about that? What do the rest of you think?"

Everyone's eyes darted around the semicircle, looking at each other. Michelle had this sense that Lucy's question was loaded, but she couldn't think of why.

"That sounds like a trick question," Andrea responded.

"Omar's right," Bill blurted out. "Anyone can see the open-source code, anyone can review it, test it. On the other hand, you're relying on a company that created the closed source. You don't know what's in their code."

"I agree," Andrea said out loud.

"Me too," said Michelle.

"Me three," said Omar.

"Well, I think you're wrong. Open source is no better than closed source, nor is it any worse. You assumed that because it was open, it was being reviewed by many other people. But that's just an assumption. You don't know it to be true. This is an example of something called 'diffusion of responsibility.'" Lucy did sound very academic.

"Wait," Omar paused his list making and spun around in his chair. "You're telling me that even though open source is open, it's no more likely to be safer than closed source?"

"That's exactly what I'm saying. That's where diffusion of responsibility comes in. Diffusion of responsibility refers to a situation where as the number of bystanders increases, the personal responsibility that an individual bystander feels decreases. As a consequence, so does their individual tendency to help. So, for an open-source project, someone using that project assumes that the project's team and other users are ensuring some level of quality. If all users of that project feel that way, effectively no one is actually reviewing anything," Lucy said.

"Lucy, it may be the hangryness or the lack of sleep, but I don't see how this is getting back to that dependency issue we're having," Michelle responded heatedly.

"Yes, the dependency. Sorry for the diversion, it's just that this is so interesting."

Omar gave Michelle a pointed look before spinning back around to his laptop. Obviously he didn't think so either.

"We think the dependency that's causing this problem is an open-source project, based on talks with our security firm. But we don't know yet if it's a software supply chain attack," Lucy explained.

"How can someone attack a supply chain?" Andrea asked.

"Issues caused by someone in the supply chain can be unintentional or nefarious," Lucy said. "For example, that vanilla we keep talking about. If the vanilla manufacturer didn't properly clean their equipment or the production line had a bacteria issue, and then all of the cakes using that manufacturer's vanilla could make people sick. This could affect people throughout the world, depending on who purchases that manufacturer's vanilla and where they are. The same is true if there was a disgruntled employee. Someone with *nefarious* intentions could poison the vanilla, causing the same issues. The outcome is still a lot of sick people," explained Lucy.

"We think it's the same with our software supply chain, like the dependency in question right now. It could be just a coding error or a bug that wasn't caught before release. But if someone nefariously introduced some malicious code in the project, then we'd have a software supply chain attack," said Lucy.

"Ah, I get it now," Andrea said. "Somehow there is a flaw with this dependency. This flaw has gone overlooked. Since everyone just trusted things were good, without validating, this flaw crept its way into our software. It reminds me of something my dad used to say: 'The road to hell is paved with good intentions.'"

"The only thing I don't understand is how could we have prevented this?" Omar said, spinning around once more and handing Lucy the very long list of affected apps. "What could we have done better? Is this something we can check for when we build our own software?"

"Perfect question!" Lucy replied. "And one I don't have an answer to."

"Hey, gang!" someone shouted across the room. "The bosses got catering for a late lunch. It's all set up in the NOC, so go get yourself a bite."

"Let's get Michelle to the front of the line. She's slowly transforming into a hangry monster," Omar said, only half joking.

Michelle quickly threw him a mean glance.

CHAPTER 10

Wednesday, September 21st

It took several weeks for the IUI team to get the supply chain problem under control. They assumed it would be an easy fix once they identified all the affected software. They were wrong.

At times, it seemed like a clear journey, although they learned the hard lesson of mistaking a clear journey for a short distance. The team had to work on it for weeks, including weekends, pulling focus away from Turbo Eureka. And they weren't the only ones. It seemed every tech organization in the world had spent the last few weeks painstakingly searching for every affected app. Michele had never experienced anything like it.

Inside IUI, calls for an outside engineering firm to come in and help with Turbo Eureka became louder. No matter what Team Kraken did, the naysayers were coming out of the woodwork, like cicadas come out, en masse, every thirteen years or so. The chastising, blaming, and sometimes name-calling began to take an emotional toll on everyone on the team, even Michelle.

She felt like she and her team had fallen from some type of grace. All the hard work and progress they had been making with the automated governance tools were suddenly forgotten as their deadline was fast approaching. They had mitigated the latest fire by patching all instances of the Java dependency, but they were no closer to solving how to avoid software supply chain vulnerabilities in the future. It started to get so bad that Michelle kept getting wind of engineers putting their resumes out, looking for other positions.

It was mid-afternoon on a Wednesday when Michelle saw Lucy walk into the dungeon. Her heart raced for a minute, worried there was a new vulnerability that was going cause another massive delay. But Lucy was all smiles.

Bill, Michelle, Barry, Andrea, and Omar were standing around two high-top tables reviewing actions for their next iteration of the Turbo Eureka automated governance tool. As she approached, Lucy jokingly said, "If only these tabletops could talk! Looks like the brain trust is hard at work."

"Loathing is more like it," Michelle replied. "We completed automating more gates for our deployment process, but we're still not feeling hot about the product. This constant talk of bringing in consultants is driving me insane."

"Yes, me too," replied Bill. "It's as if they're asking on repeat as a way to wear me out. All with the hopes that one day my response will be 'Yes, they'll be here tomorrow.' And then, magically, all our problems will vanish with a flick of their magical consultant wands."

"I've been doing some reading on software supply chain analysis tools," Lucy said. "I'm almost convinced that something more can be done as part of your automated governance that would help in future supply chain-related issues. Have you thought about generating a valid SBOM as a gate for your continuous integration?" Lucy asked.

"An S bomb? Is that like an F bomb?" Omar asked.

"It stands for software bill of materials. SBOM."

"No, we haven't," Michelle replied. "But I've begun to hear that term more and more."

"Well, enlighten me, please," Omar said.

Lucy responded, "It's simply a list of all the components you use to build your software, like the one that caused all our issues not too long ago."

"Don't remind me," Michelle groaned.

"Really, that's all it is? Heck, we already have that. It's called a POM[1] file in Java if you build with Maven," Omar replied without caring to explain further.

"Mmm, yes and no . . ." Lucy equivocated.

"What?! A POM file is exactly the same thing. How am I wrong?" Omar questioned, as if Lucy was on trial.

"Well, the idea has been around for a while, although its initial incarnations were simply as a way to track licenses for software components," Lucy continued without directly answering Omar's question. "Recently, with the rise in exploits of supply chain vulnerability issues, the concept of a software bill of materials is a thing as well as a rally cry to people across industry. It's an attempt to raise awareness about the quality of software, and most of the zeal has been aimed at open-source software. But honestly, if you ask me, I think too many people are trying to use it as a silver bullet.

"According to the US Department of Commerce, an SBOM is a formal, machine-readable inventory of software components and dependencies, information about those components, and their hierarchical relationships. On May 12th, 2021, the President of the United States issued an executive order on improving

---

1. A Project Object Model or POM is a unit of work in Maven. It consists of an XML file containing information about the project as well as configuration details used by Maven to build the project.

the nation's cyber security.[2] The executive order specifically calls out commercial software providers to provide an SBOM, so that federal or regulated entities are able to quickly identify vulnerabilities or threats from the dependencies used in commercial software. It also enables companies using commercial software to attest software before it's installed."

"Okay, but you still haven't told me why I'm wrong," Omar rebutted.

"An SBOM is an extensive list of all software components and dependencies. Omar, from your perspective, for someone who is writing an application, it would be not only the list of dependencies you primarily depend upon, like the ones in your POM file. It would be a list of all the transitive dependencies, including extra information such as version numbers and where that dependency came from. It's your full dependency tree, a full *family tree* of what uses what, all the way down to the roots."

"Oh . . . that's a bit more complicated," Omar said in surrender.

Lucy continued, "It doesn't end there. I think the SBOM should include the machine the software is running on, the version of the operating system running on that machine, where that machine is located, and so on, even down to the other software running on that machine alongside yours."

"Isn't that what our Configuration Management Database does?" Bill asked.

"The CMDB?!" Lucy said with a full belly laugh. "Setting my true feelings aside for a CMDB, Bill, sort of. The idea of the CMDB is to logically lay out how software and hardware assets interact with each other. The problem with a CMDB is it's generally out of date the moment it's updated. I'm not sure I've ever been in a company where you could truly trust it. Most of the time, it was the best guess at what our technology landscape looked like, but it was never 100% correct. And I'm not talking about a little off—it's generally way off."

Bill responded, "Okay, how the CMDB is maintained may be an issue, but in concept it's similar, right?"

"Yes, I'll concede that."

"So, how do we go about generating an SBOM?" Omar asked. "That's a ton of information that might be hard to get. And who's going to do it? Who has time?"

Lucy replied, "Does your software composition analysis tool not do this for you? They may not explicitly call it an SBOM; they'll most likely call it a *dependency tree* or a *dependency analysis*. Usually the tool will check your tree of dependencies to see if there are any CVEs for that specific dependency and version."

"Actually, it does. We're using this report for the SCA[3] quality gate of our automated governance right now," Michelle replied.

---

2. See more on US Executive Order on Improving the Nation's Cybersecurity in Appendix 6.
3. See Appendix 5 for a detailed explanation of software component analyses (SCAs).

"That's great to hear. There are industry agreed-upon formats like CycloneDX or SPDX. It wouldn't be too hard to create an SBOM in one of those formats from that data," Lucy replied.

"Hold up, this isn't making any sense. Lucy, you're telling us to do something we're already doing, which is checking for vulnerabilities at build time with the SCA tool?" Omar interjected.

"Close. You can't just scan a dependency once. At the time you scanned the dependency there may have been no vulnerabilities. That's simply because no one was aware. A new vulnerability may be published any time, and unless you build your application at least once after that you won't know about the vulnerability. The problem with how lots of folks use SCA is that the scan happens only during a build that is triggered by a code change," Lucy replied.

"Ohhhh," Omar said as his eyes lit up. "I get it! Old software that we're running on our machines but not developing anymore might have vulnerabilities. And we wouldn't know because we haven't scanned them recently!"

Omar paused, reflected on his own observation, and involuntarily shuddered. Snapping out of it, he asked, "Okay, but how does this all tie back to the SBOM again?"

"Well, the SBOM is a list of all dependencies, as we discussed before. So instead of always rebuilding software just to scan, you can simply scan the SBOMs for all newly published vulnerabilities and know if there are impacts. You can also use this to proactively upgrade old dependencies or replace vulnerable ones used in multiple locations or products," Lucy stated.

"Okay, so an SBOM is like a map. When something new happens to a dependency, a new CVE for example, we can easily locate it on the map and see what roads lead to and from it. Then, with this information, we can take some action to address it," Omar said.

"Yes," Lucy replied. "We like to refer to this as detective versus preventative controls. Preventative controls are things we do to prevent something bad from moving forward. These are what our build-time quality gates are responsible for. Then there are detective controls. Detective controls are things, like an SBOM, we can do to validate a system is still in compliance as the things around the system change, like the dependencies. Your running software itself will not change while in production, but an exploit could be identified. With checking for compliance at rest and at runtime, we can detect these new situations."

"That gives me an idea," Omar said. "I've been playing with this new graph database. I bet I could create something that stores the dependency list from the SCA tool and give the ability for us to search for a dependency. That way, if something like this happens again, we can just query for the dependency and see what the affected systems are."

"Oh, I like this," Michelle said, her eyes widening in excitement. "I'm always keeping on the engineers to update their latest dependencies. I can use this to identify who needs to keep their stuff up to date. I bet we can also apply some analytics to the SBOM data to finally help us rationalize what technologies our teams are using to build our software and be more intentional about what frameworks we're placing our bets on!"

"Maybe this isn't such a good idea," Omar responded, tongue-in-cheek. "But seriously, give me about a week and I can have an MVP put together for us."[4]

Friday, September 30th

In usual fashion, what was supposed to be a week turned into nearly two weeks.

It was Friday morning, and Michelle was huddled over Omar's desk. He had finished the prototype late last night and wanted Michelle to be the first set of eyes on it.

"Look up CVE-2020-17530 and see what comes back," Michelle asked him.

"Oh, wow—unless my prototype is buggy, that's a lot of results," Omar replied.

"No, that doesn't surprise me. I'll fill you in later. Let's demo this. I'll grab the others," Michelle said as she ran off.

About thirty minutes later they were all gathered around the high-tops in the dungeon. Bill was the last to arrive.

"Hello everyone," Michelle said.

"Unless Omar is telling fairy tales, it sounds like you all have made some good progress," Bill said.

"I think we have, but we'll let you be the judge. Check out our SBOM approach," Michelle responded, turning to Omar.

Omar proceeded to walk everyone through their continuous integration process so far. He rushed through gates such as code review and unit testing. He hurried to the software composition analysis gate. Omar added the SBOM procedure after the SCA gate. When the SCA gate passed, this subsequent procedure took the dependency tree and created a new record of it in Omar's graph database. Once this was done, the rest of the continuous integration process continued as normal.

Omar turned back to the rest of the group and explained that with the interface he provided, when a new CVE is issued, anyone can simply enter the information about the dependency inquisition, then click *Search*. To demonstrate it, he pulled up

---

4. OWASP's Dependency Track,is a popular open source SBOM management platform that allows organizations to identify and reduce risk in their software supply chain.

a new web browser on his computer and went to the new demo SBOM Search site that he created and entered *CVE-2020-17530*. Numerous results came back.

"Here are the applications that are impacted by this CVE. You're seeing not only what applications use this as a primary dependency but also those that have this as a transitive dependency."

Bill looked at Barry. "What does this mean for Security?"

"It's risk mitigation. Think of it as continuous monitoring, just like we do in the NOC. What Omar showed is how we can continuously search through the bits and pieces that make up our applications to identify a bad part, then see what other parts of the system they affect. It reduces our mean time to act in the face of a vulnerability or exploit caused by a software dependency."

"It's really the epitome of real-time supply chain compliance," Andrea added. "For this type of situation, we can assess, at a moment's notice, what our risk exposure is to any identified software supply chain vulnerability. Whereas before, we'd just repeat the mistakes we made over a month ago. Now, we can identify affected systems within seconds and enact control procedures to mitigate any risk. In addition to this, we can now get proactive with our risk management. As each of these components has new versions available, we can use this to identify all the systems that need to be updated to the newest version. Keeping our software dependencies updated with the latest version releases is a leading way to mitigate risk. We can now enforce compliance at build time, rest time, and run time."

Barry turned to Omar, "Is this hooked up to our CMDB?"

Omar, with a flushed face, responded, "No, it's not. That was not the best approach."

Barry seemed to get visibly flustered. "Why not? It seems that this is exactly why we have a configuration management database!"

"Searchability is key," Omar replied. "I don't want to go into too much detail, but our CMDB has limited search capabilities and can't be used in this problem. I used sophisticated graph search algorithms for this. "

"Kid, I did my computer science degree forty years ago. I try to stay current but I'm not following the graph search algorithm reasoning. You're saying we can't do that with our CMDB?" Barry replied.

"Okay, sorry, " Omar said in an apologetic tone. "But yes, our CMDB can't handle this. With a depth-first search, we can take a piece of software we wrote and ask, 'Does this software have a dependency upon X?' The depth-first search will traverse all the dependencies of the dependencies of the dependencies to find out if the dependency in question is being used, either as a primary or a transitive dependency. It's the same type of problem you'd come across if you were navigating a maze. Depth-first helps navigate a maze-like question. Does that make sense?"

"Yes, it's starting to come back now," Barry replied.

"Well then," Omar continued, "with a breadth-first search, we can ask, 'What software uses dependency X?' It's similar to what web crawlers do for search engines or when you ask your GPS 'Where are all restaurants located around me?' Each of these methods provide us a way to analyze our software dependency relationships across differing software bills of materials created for our systems. Our CMDB doesn't do this."

Barry didn't know what to say. It was as if Omar politely called his kid ugly, and Barry wanted to agree that his kid was ugly.

"Okay. This is great everyone. What we've just seen here is simply impressive. Omar, I understand it's just a prototype, but if we can get this into production as soon as possible, we have something really special here." Bill sounded very happy.

"Agreed," Andrea said.

"We need to update the external audit team on our progress, and it's time to give the regulators another update. Omar, Michelle, I want you both ready to give a full presentation to stakeholders next week. Andrea, can you brief Jada and get her up to speed?"

"Will do," Andrea responded, as they all stood up to leave.

CHAPTER 11

Thursday, October 6th

Michelle and Omar were nervous. It was now time to meet with IUI executives to show their progress. The target deadline for completing Turbo Eureka was only five months away. All the executives were eager to show the regulators that they had made sufficient progress to put the MRAs to bed and get IUI out of the doghouse, so to speak.

The meeting was a who's who of IUI tech leadership: Jada King (CRCO), Tim Jones (CISO), Jennifer Limus (CIO/VP of Engineering), and of course, Jason Colbert (SVP of Digital Transformation).

With all of the criticism and pressure they had experienced from the supply chain issue, Michelle didn't want this demo to come off as a failure. After all, it was a conceptual prototype. It wasn't meant for production in its current state. She was all too aware that some of the people watching this demo were the ones casting criticism and calling for an outside engineering firm. If this fell flat on its face, there would be more pain coming the team's way.

Michelle opened up the meeting by referencing the original demo of project Turbo Eureka and explaining that in the weeks since their initial prototype, Team Kraken had developed it even further to include support for new policies and address the recent supply chain break.

Michelle shared her screen with the attendees and started to run through the same steps from the first demo, opening a pull request from a feature branch and requesting an approval from Omar. She then pulled up a visual of the CI pipeline, which showed a series of steps:

1. Code Checkout (30 sec)
2. Sign and Build (2 min)
3. Unit Test (1 min)
4. Static Code Quality Scan (2 min)
5. SCA (Software Composition Analysis) (2 min)
6. SBOM (Software Bill of Materials) (1 min)
7. Static Security Test (9 min)

8. Publish (1 min)

9. Update Manifest (45 sec)

Michelle knew from experience that a nearly twenty-minute pipeline demo was just about as exciting as watching paint dry. To make sure her audience didn't lose interest, she kicked off the pipeline and then gave a play by play to highlight how each of the policies would be enforced during the demo.

"Okay, everyone, the excitement begins! I've just kicked off the pipeline. In real life, the build will be triggered by our Git tool when a pull request is merged. I am doing it manually just for the demo. The CI build is validating that the code build is successful and that it follows our enterprise policies and standards for building and publishing a deployable artifact. By artifact, of course, I mean the actual application code that is compiled and ready to run.

"Next," she said while gesturing with her hand at the code review notes on the screen, "the code review here captures all code changes and verifies that all changes to the release branch were made via the pull request. It also verifies that each pull request received at least one approval from someone other than the code author. It's important to note that we can adjust how many approvals any change needs without having to rebuild the whole thing from scratch."

There was a series of small nods around the room.

"Now, I want to highlight that this branching pattern confirms that the application team practiced our enterprise-approved branching pattern when committing changes to the code repository. For all microservice applications, IUI requires that developers practice either trunk-based development[1] or use short-lived feature branches. Prior to this, our teams used complex non-standard branching patterns, and we always ran into erroneous deployments—every now and then, wrong versions of code showed up in production!

"Next is the code signature policy gate. It verifies the checksum of every artifact. This check ensures that each artifact was digitally signed at build time, confirming that it was created in a trusted IUI build environment.

"Once that is complete, we move to the unit test policy gate. The unit tests confirm the successful execution and code coverage of the application's unit tests. IUI has minimum code coverage standards, but we all believe that each product development team should determine their minimum standard, which is above and beyond IUI standard.

"Next, we have the code quality policy gate. The third-party tool we use for code quality ensures that we have reliable, maintainable, and simple code. This gate

---

1. Trunk–based development is a source-control branching model in which developers work on code in a single branch called the 'trunk.' Learn more here: https://trunkbaseddevelopment.com/

ensures that the quality scores we receive from this tool meet or exceed IUI standards for new code.

"The next gate is SCA, or software composition analysis, which is the automated process to identify all open-source software usage. IUI uses this information to ensure all open-source software used meets IUI technology standards, is free from vulnerabilities, and is using licenses that are approved by IUI's legal department.

"Right after the SCA gate, we use the raw data from SCA, produce a version of a software bill of materials and save it on our SBOM Database. Please note that this may be a temporary solution. We will probably use an open-source solution in the future.

"Now we're at the Static Security Test policy gate. This stage in the pipeline ensures that there are no critical or high vulnerabilities in the source code. We also have special rules to identify any user credentials or keys exposed in the source code."

By the time Michelle finished walking through each of the new policies, the pipeline build had concluded. A new artifact was published in the deployment repository and the manifest file updated with a new version number. She turned her attention back to her laptop and navigated to the demo application's source code repository, where she eagerly displayed the source code repository's README file with a shields.io badge for each of the policy checks she had just described.

Demo App

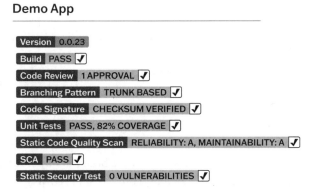

"Done! Look at that! All the policy gates are green." The meeting attendees were silent, although they stared intently at the monitor mirroring Michelle's screen. Some people squinted as if they were deep in thought, while others glanced around at their peers. Michelle looked over at Carol with surprise. She had expected the audience to be considerably more thrilled. Perhaps some of the leaders didn't understand what they had just seen.

Michelle had an idea. "Let me show you what happens if a developer breaks one of the policies," she said, betting that the stoppage of an artifact in violation of policy might resonate better with the less-than-technical leadership.

Her fingers crunched her laptop keys while her eyes darted back and forth between the audience and her screen. She was trying to keep their attention while she rushed to orchestrate a shortened rerun of the build pipeline. "Alright, now look at this!" she exclaimed. "I pushed a code change without approvals and ran the pipeline on my local machine instead of the IUI build servers." She pointed to the large monitor in the meeting room that mirrored her laptop screen. Several of the previously green badges had turned red. "See the badges?"

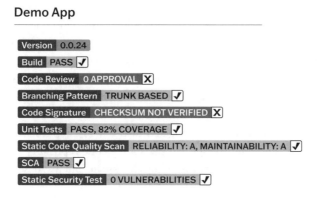

Michelle explained that her second code change, which she pushed directly to the main branch of the source code repository without a pull request, failed the code review policy and showed a red badge with a large X. Murmurs of comprehension came from the audience. Michelle grinned—it was starting to click.

She then pointed out the *Code Signature* badge and explained that because she was running the build on her laptop and not an IUI-approved pipeline instance, the digital code signature did not match.

The audience looked puzzled, so Carol jumped in to summarize. "If the signatures don't match, that means the code may have been built by an untrusted and potentially malicious build environment. If we can't trust the environment that built the code, we also cannot trust the code itself."

"And what exactly makes you trust your build environment?" Tim quickly interjected.

"I knew you were going to ask that question, Tim." Michelle had a smile on her face. "Your team has actually scanned and tested our build server and build agent software. We store this approved software in a binary repository. For every build, we pull down the approved build agent software, instantiate the agent to create the build environment, run the build, and destroy the instance. Of course, we confirm that the hash of the build server and its build agent match the expected hash, so we can be confident no one tampered with it."

"Oh wow! I didn't know that. I'm so happy that my team was thoroughly engaged with your team throughout this." Tim looked very pleased.

"So, going back to the failures . . . what happens now? Do those failures break the pipeline?" Tim asked.

"Well, yes and no," Michelle responded. "They will cause the deployment pipeline job to fail."

Tim, annoyed by the seemingly anal-retentive correction, responded, "Okay, what's the difference?"

"So at IUI we have CI and CD, or as I refer to them, build and deploy. The build pipeline takes code and compiles it to a binary artifact, which is published to our internal artifact repository. And then the deploy pipeline takes that artifact off the artifact repository and deploys it onto a server or wherever the thing can run."

"And a red badge results in a failed *deploy* pipeline?" Tim asked.

"Yes, exactly!"

"I'm confused," he responded. "Shouldn't a component be considered 'deployed' when it reaches the internal artifact repository?"

"No, you're thinking of 'publish,'" Omar interjected. "The publish stage pushes to the artifact repository, which happens at the end of the build pipeline. The deploy pipeline is a whole different thing."

"But what about shared libraries?" Tim asked.

Omar didn't expect such a targeted rebuttal. "What do you mean?" he asked.

"A Java or NPM library, something like that." Tim folded his arms, leaned back, and crossed his legs. "Those aren't directly deployed to a server, but they're used by other applications, so they're still reaching production. In that scenario, isn't the 'publish' stage considered the deployment?"

"Well, it depends on your definition of deployment," Michelle conceded.

"I consider an artifact deployed when it becomes consumable, either by the customer or other applications," Tim said.

"Okay, now *I'm* confused," Jada exclaimed. "I thought a deployment meant a new set of features were being delivered to customers."

"That's called a release," said Omar.

"I think we're talking past one another," said Carol.

"We are," said Jennifer, as she stood up and reached for a dry-erase marker. "For the sake of this conversation, let's use the following definitions . . ."

She spelled out three definitions on the board:

- **Build**—compile the code, publish binary to artifact repository.
- **Deploy**—push a new version of the app onto the server.
- **Release**—a mechanism that allows end user to access new features or functionalities in the new version of the application.

"For this conversation, can we all agree on these definitions?" asked Jennifer.

Tim was not convinced that his question on shared libraries was answered yet. He felt there was an unmitigated risk there. In his mind he was convinced that the shared libraries should be going through the same compliance checks before any application teams were allowed to use them. But he didn't want to disrupt the flow either.

"Okay, I am good with this. For now. But I need your team to have a backlog item to revisit this shared library scenario," Tim said. "You can consult my team any time if you need help. Does that sound alright?"

Everyone nodded.

Carol continued. "Great. Now if a control is failing, why wouldn't the pipeline just break the build?"

Michelle looked puzzled.

"Why not just break the build? That would alleviate the need to distinguish which code bases are consumed after *publish* or *deploy*," Jennifer asserted.

Jennifer was persuasive, but Michelle countered, "What if there's an emergency? When a team builds their code it could be a break-glass situation. In that situation, a failed build could lead to a disaster."

Carol interjected, "I think what Michelle is saying is that it seems draconian to fail a build for a missing code review. And what if there's an emergency? Do we really want to be so strict that we can't allow individual teams to use their discretion?"

Jada leaned forward. "So let me confirm my understanding. You're saying that you want to build and publish all applications to the internal artifact repository, regardless of their compliance."

"But—" Omar tried to interject but resigned to Jada.

"But you're going to allow—" Jada took a breath, frustrated that she had to keep digging to get the answer she was looking for. "Who is going to be the one to decide whether to deploy a non-compliant application?"

"I don't know. That can be up to you. We just want to make sure that someone can accept the risk," Carol responded. "Let's just finish the demo and then we can discuss at the end."

"Sure," said Jada. "But can I ask one more question while we're on this?"

"Of course." Carol was in fact happy that Jada was fully engaged in the demo.

"Where are you storing all these data?" Jada asked.

"Let me take that one," Omar finally interjected. "We store the data in a database, and we call that an evidence store. Only Team Kraken has access to the evidence store."

"Is that how it's going to be in the future?" It was clear that Jada was not fully onboard with the idea that an engineering team would still have control over the evidence store.

"Well, we can talk about the ownership when we are through the crisis," Carol replied. "I do understand where you're coming from, Jada. If your team wants to control the admin access to that evidence store, we can make that happen. We didn't know if you would have someone who can administer it . . ."

"That's true," Jada nodded. "I'll have to think about that some more but please continue."

Michelle navigated to the demo app's deployment repository and pointed out the version of the artifact: *iui-demo-app:0.0.24*.

She opened a pull request from the staging branch to the dev branch, indicating the intention of deploying to the dev environment. Carol approved the pull request, and the deployment pipeline kicked off before failing abruptly. Michelle turned around to face the large monitor in the meeting room and pointed to the deploy pipeline logs at the bottom of the screen.

```
2021-05-04 11:01:01   CHECKING OUT HTTPS://GIT.INVESTMENTSUNLIMITEDBANK.COM;KRAKEN/IUI-DEMO/COMMIT/9A6E39
2021-05-04 11:01:02
2021-05-04 11:01:03   VERIFYING POLICY FOR IUI-DEMO-APP:0.0.24
2021-05-04 11:01:04
2021-05-04 11:01:05   IUI-DEMO-APP:0.0.24 FAILED THE FOLLOWING POLICIES ["CODE REVIEW", "CODE SIGNATURE"]
2021-05-04 11:01:06
2021-05-04 11:01:07   DEPLOYMENT FAILED, PLEASE CREATE A SUPPORT TICKET BEFORE OPENING AN INCIDENT
2021-05-04 11:01:08   HTTPS://HTTPS://DEVELOPER.INVESTMENTSUNLIMITEDBANK.COM//HELP
```

"See? Right there! It failed," she looked back to the audience to gauge their reactions, happy to see that her audience was visibly pleased by her team's work.

"This is great," volunteered Jada, who was clearly enjoying this demo but was also somewhat puzzled. "But I have to admit I assumed this type of thing was already happening. Was I naive?"

"There was no automation to ensure our policies," Michelle replied, "and to be honest, nobody was actually doing all of this manually either. We were not doing what we said we were doing. Hence the MRIA that has brought us all here." Michelle meant it as a bit of a joke to lighten the mood, but no one even smiled.

"Uh," Michelle continued, "when the policies are dependent upon manual validation, there is a risk that steps will be skipped. This automation ensures that we aren't missing the required steps. Additionally, we just made the right way easy. We paved the road, if you will. And when you make the right way easy, people tend to do the right thing."

"I have a feeling that our developers will love this," Jada exclaimed. "This is a much better developer experience; do it automatically, do it early, and fail fast."

"There is one thing that we did not demo here," Michelle said, "and that's testing—automated functional and performance testing that we perform. A couple of years ago we developed a modern test automation platform using open-source technologies. We named it Orion. This platform allows teams to run automated tests, captures test results, and runs many reports that teams use before production deployment."

"Do we need to change anything in there?" Jada asked.

"I don't think so. To be honest, that is the only platform that does what it's supposed to do. Developers like it, and as far as I can tell, all of IUI uses it," Jennifer replied convincingly.

"Anyway, that is what we have so far. Any questions?" Michelle was relieved that the demo went as she had expected.

"This is great, team. Wow—just great," Jada said, before redirecting the conversation. "But can we go back to the topic of accepting risk?"

"Sure," said Carol. "Where did we leave off?"

Jada briefly glanced at her notes. "In a scenario where a control fails, who makes the decision of 'go' or 'no go,' and what controls have we placed on that process?"

"Ultimately the application owner or the product owner will make the decision to accept the risk, and Risk, Change, whoever else can monitor those decisions. That stuff we can work out later," Carol responded, "but for now may I propose a workflow?"

"Let's hear it," said Jada.

Carol uncapped a dry-erase marker and rolled her chair over to the board.

"As we all know, when a team goes to deploy, they need a change record. Teams are currently expected to manually upload evidence to the CMDB to satisfy required policies."

"Yes, okay," Jada said.

"I propose that Turbo Eureka orchestrates the creation of this change record during the promote stage of the deployment process. By doing so, it allows each attestation to populate the change record so that the final reviewer—the application owner—has the opportunity to view the proposed change and the current state of compliance."

Omar took a breath before speaking up. "And—"

"Hang on Omar, just a second," replied Carol. She continued, "By creating the change record directly from the pipeline, we can ensure that the proper artifact versions are documented, as well as the compliance status for each. So when the application owner reviews the change prior to deployment and sees failed controls, he or she can choose to accept the risk or reject the change. Turbo Eureka's automation will allow them to make that decision."

Satisfied with the synopsis of Carol's proposal, Jada exclaimed, "I love it. I mean, anything you can do to accelerate that process will be a tremendous success. But, I don't want to speak for our partners in change management, so please be sure to bring them along as you build this out."

"Of course," said Carol.

"So what happens if they're not failing any compliance check?" asked Jennifer. She already knew the answer that she wanted to hear, but she often employed the Socratic method to steer the conversation.

"Right! Thank you, I almost forgot," said Carol. "We want to incentivize teams. We want to make the right thing the easy thing, agreed?"

Jada nodded.

Carol continued, "So if a change is submitted with 100% compliance, let's eliminate CAB."[2]

"What do you mean when you say *eliminate*?" asked Jada.

"You're preapproved. No paperwork or meetings required," Carol replied.

Jada leaned back but didn't respond. It was evident that Carol's proposal had caused her to pause for a moment and think.

"You're not proposing to completely disband CAB, are you?" Jada was trying to grasp the full impact of this in the future.

"Well, I sure would like to explore if we can at least skip the CAB meetings!" Carol wanted to thoughtfully choose her words. "Even the CAB members feel that the meetings don't add value. They also know the meetings become the bottleneck for teams that want to deploy more frequently."

"I can see how this can completely change how we think about CAB." Jada had the 'thinking out loud' expression on her face. "We can actually arm CAB with more real-time, trustworthy data for them to act only when it's needed. They can be consulting partners rather than an approval authority. I'm seeing win-win all over the place!"

"Exactly!" Michelle jumped in. "Application or product owners can reach out to CAB members if they have questions or need guidance before accepting any risk."

For a brief moment the room fell silent.

Sensing an opening and a chance to redirect the conversation, Tim asked, "How many teams in IUI are using Turbo Eureka right now?"

Michelle replied, "Right now, just one team."

Tim responded, "Well, that doesn't do us any good, does it?" He gestured to the large monitor across the room. "I love what you all have built here and I think it's really slick. But we need to focus on onboarding more apps to this platform instead of adding new policies and features." He continued, "We can't satisfy regulators with only one team following the new system. Remind me, how many TLCs do we have here at IUI?"

TLC stood for three-letter code. The codes were used as unique identifiers to keep inventory of different technology assets throughout IUI. Unsure of the answer,

---

2. The CAB (Change Advisory Board) is a group of people responsible for prioritizing and scheduling changes.

Michelle looked around for help. When nobody indicated that they knew the answer, Carol offered a response, "I think we have somewhere around 1,900 code repositories."

"That's not what I'm asking," Tim said. "How many TLCs do we have in our CMDB?"

Carol jumped in. "We have 587," she said.

Tim glanced at his watch. "Alright, we're over time. I want to know what the plan is to onboard all 587 TLCs. Bonus credit if you can also quickly put together a way to prevent any new TLCs from being created without this capability. Let's pick it up there when we meet next week."

Friday, October 7th

Michelle, Carol, Omar, and the rest of Team Kraken reconvened the following morning to debrief on the stakeholder demo the day before. Barry and Andrea also joined.

"I just wanted to say how impressed I am with the progress that you're making. The demo yesterday was very exciting. And you all know I don't say things like that lightly," Bill said before continuing to the topic he really wanted to discuss. "Now, let's talk about making it available for others. How are we going to onboard 587 TLCs, and fast?"

He looked around the table, inviting the whole team to participate.

Omar jumped at the opportunity to speak up. "Five hundred and eighty-seven is a meaningless number! Some TLCs have one code repository and others have tens. Some are IUI-developed software applications, but most of them are either infra-structure or COTS applications—uh, that's commercial off-the-shelf . . ." Omar explained, turning to Andrea.

"I actually knew that one, but thanks," Andrea replied in a whisper.

Michelle picked up on Omar's point and attempted to expand on it. "I think what we're saying is that the first iteration of Turbo Eureka is designed for software that's developed in house. So we should probably focus our onboarding efforts there."

"We also need to prioritize any of the apps called out in the original MRAs," Andrea added. "And anything high to moderate risk, like internet facing, customer service, and so on."

Omar nodded in agreement.

Michelle continued, "After yesterday's meeting, I combed through each of the 587 TLCs in the CMDB and identified any that indicated they contained custom,

IUI-developed software components. After filtering out the rest, I was left with a list of 183 that are eligible. I believe this is the list we need to use for onboarding."

"Only 183?" Barry responded. "Do we trust the numbers in our CMDB? In any case, I don't think Tim is going to be happy to hear that you only plan to cover 183 TLCs. Carol, I thought you said that IUI had over 1,900 code repositories. How does that align with this list of 183?"

"Some TLCs have more than one code repository. Think of a code repository like it represents a component of TLC. But on the other hand, some repositories do not belong to any TLCs," Michelle tried to clarify, but she only ended up introducing more confusion.

"How do we not know how many code repositories actually belong to TLCs?" Barry was getting irritated.

"Well, anybody can create a code repository, and some of them choose to include their TLC number in the name. We require any repository that builds using a standard pipeline to declare the TLC number in their build file."

"That's it!" Barry exclaimed. "We know it!"

"But there's no requirement that your repository must use the standard pipeline." Omar rolled his eyes and continued, "Many teams use their own stuff."

"Duh!" Barry almost gave up in frustration. "So make a new rule—repositories must be named after the TLCs."

"The last thing we need is rules around naming repositories. This place is already way more restrictive than any tech company I've ever worked for."

"I don't disagree with you. But what are you going to use for onboarding?" Carol asked.

"I think I hate CMDB!" Omar looked away. "And I hate TLCs too. Why do we have to use them for anything? Why do we care?"

"Omar! We have to use the TLCs. And the CMDB too! The change tickets for production releases are generated by CMDB and are issued against TLCs." Michelle tried to calm Omar down.

"We're almost at time, and I have a 10:30 that I need to be at," said Barry, turning to Carol. "Carol, as you know, Security is very interested in knowing how Turbo Eureka will be rolled out. As is the entire board, frankly. We still need to show the regulators that we're doing what we say we're doing. This group has built a great tool. I just want to make sure it's successful. Tim has told me this is his top priority."

"Of course," said Carol.

After Barry and Carol left the meeting, Omar got up to close the door. When he sat back down he sighed. "So what are we going to do?" he asked.

When no one answered immediately, Dillon said, "Last year one of the contractors wrote a script to comb through repositories and capture metadata for an internal audit. He's gone, but I think I know where he kept it. It won't be perfect, but what if we used that to onboard?"

"That still won't solve the problem of identifying the TLC numbers," Michelle reminded him.

"I guess not," Dillon responded.

"Hmm," Omar said, perking up, "what if we ingest their build file and use that to get the TLC? If there's no build file, then it's not being built in the pipeline. If we block everything without a valid checksum from deploying, then we can safely assume that anything without a build file cannot be deployed, and therefore we don't need to onboard it."

"I like it!" Michelle exclaimed. "You try it out."

That afternoon, Omar found the contractor's script and executed it against IUI's source code management system. It produced 1,204 of the 1,900 code repositories at IUI, which meant that over 700 repositories were not using a standard pipeline.

The next day the team and Carol reconvened. Carol opened up the discussion. "Omar's script produced 1,204 results, which seems accurate. But it took over 45 minutes to run."

"The contractor's script," Omar clarified with a wink and a smile. He did not want to be known for writing inefficient code.

"Yes, thanks Omar, the *contractor's* script. It actually put strain on the source code platform. Many developers called the help desk saying they couldn't push code during the time the script was running. This isn't going to be a sustainable solution."

"What if we ran it each night?" Omar offered, although his body language conveyed that even he wasn't thrilled with the solution he just proposed.

"We can do better," said Carol. "I know we can. What are other ideas?"

"So we somehow need to capture the TLCs and onboard them onto Turbo Eureka . . . " Omar was thinking out loud.

"What about this?" Michelle began to share her screen, which showed a colorful body of text against the dark background of her code editor. "Here's an example of the data we're capturing during the 'checkout' stage of the build pipeline. It contains all of the environment variables, including the TLC number as well as the repository information. What if we added some custom code into the 'checkout' stage that automatically onboards the application to Turbo Eureka? That way, our inventory is updated in real time."

"That's a great idea! Screw the contractor's script," Omar said cheekily. "I know exactly how we can do that."

Monday, October 17th

A week later, Michelle's automated onboarding idea was working. Turbo Eureka went from monitoring a single application component to monitoring over sixty components across five TLCs. Since it was fully dependent on when the corresponding build would run, it would take some time for all 183 TLCs to be onboarded, but it was still an elegant solution that showed steady growth in onboarding. However, the ones that didn't use standard pipeline would still remain out of Turbo Eureka.

This made Carol and Jennifer somewhat happy because they could show consistent progress to Tim, Jada, and the external audit team on a weekly basis. It also meant Team Kraken could go back to focusing on building out more policy features in Turbo Eureka.

CHAPTER 12

Tuesday, December 13th

After two months of steady growth, the onboarding progress had stalled. At their weekly meeting, Barry pointed to a chart that one of his associates created with data pulled from the Turbo Eureka API.

"You see? It's leveling out. Right there," he said as he pointed to the right side of the chart, which depicted a linear growth in onboarding numbers until the last two weeks, when the slope of the line turned horizontal. "You all were making such great progress, but now I'm concerned."

To date, Turbo Eureka had onboarded over 850 components across 94 TLCs. It was impressive progress, but Barry was right—the numbers were leveling off and the team didn't know why.

Michelle and Omar looked at each other in dismay.

"What do you think it could be?" Omar whispered.

Michelle shrugged.

After the meeting, Michelle darted back to her desk. She knew that applications were being built because it was one of the busiest times of the year for IUI, so it didn't make sense that their onboarding had leveled off.

Michelle remembered that IUI's CI platform stored some build data in a database. A few years ago the platform team hired a few contractors to implement basic platform monitoring. As a part of that work, the contractors installed some custom scripts on the platform that shipped a subset of the raw data to an external database. She opened a high-priority service ticket to get an extract of the data for the past six months.

As a hands-on technical person, Michelle never shied away from ad hoc coding and scripting to get her work done. She opened up Jupyter notebook and after half an hour or so, she had her notebook ready with some Python code to analyze the data extract.

Two hours later, Michelle received the data extract download link from the platform team and ran her code. While looking at the charts, she muttered to herself, "That's interesting," and then she headed to Carol's office.

"Carol, take a look at this," Michelle said. She walked Carol through her findings that showed that Turbo Eureka had only captured about 60% of the builds that occurred in the pipeline since they implemented the automated onboarding feature. "As I looked through the missed builds, I noticed a trend. See the pipeline library that they're using? That's the old pipeline library."

"The *old* pipeline library?" Omar looked confused. "I didn't know we had an *old* one."

"Yes," Carol said. She had been at IUI longer than Michelle or Omar. "The enterprise standard pipeline library was part of IUI's original digital transformation six years ago. One of the primary efforts was to establish a standard across the enterprise for building and deploying code. Adoption of this standard library was very slow until two years ago, when an internal audit began pressing for teams to comply with enterprise standards. But, as this data shows, some application teams are still on the legacy pipeline."

The applications that Michelle's data identified to be using the legacy pipeline library were unable to migrate to the enterprise standard because their code bases were old, in some cases over fifteen years old. These required highly tailored build scripts that were so specific that the pipeline development team didn't have the resources to migrate them to the new standard. These applications, deemed "legacy," were not required to migrate to the new enterprise standard pipeline library, and therefore remained out of reach for onboarding.

Thursday, December 15th

Later that week, members of Team Kraken presented the findings to Barry and Tim.

Recently, Security had taken an even keener interest in Turbo Eureka. After Turbo Eureka's early successes, they started seeing opportunities for reducing the less-scalable manual processes that had been employed through the years.

"I've been giving regular updates to Tim on your progress, and he's here today to help remove anything that may be blocking you." Barry turned to his boss. "Tim, as you know, I've worked very closely with Michelle and her team through the development phase and now during the onboarding. I'm here to make sure that we're all communicating with one another and that the expectations of each team are clear."

Omar rolled his eyes, as Barry always seemed to make himself the hero when his boss was in the room.

Carol opened up by giving the context of the previous meeting. She recalled that the team took an action item to review pipeline data for possible explanations as to why automated onboarding had stalled. When it was her turn, Michelle explained her findings that an unknown number of components across an estimated eighty-nine TLCs were still using the old pipeline library.

She began to explain that during the digital transformation, all applications were expected to move to the new shared pipeline library, but applications that were deemed "legacy" were allowed to continue using the old pipelines. An estimated eighty-nine TLCs were still using the old pipelines that were built five or six years ago.

Carol started by saying how Michelle and her team tried to get to the bottom of some onboarding discrepancies that they were seeing. She then went on to explain why the auto-onboarding process is failing in some cases.

"Can we stop right here?" Tim said, exhibiting frustration at the growing intricacies of the conversation. "What's the total number here? How many TLC numbers have been onboarded?"

"Almost a hundred," Omar proudly responded.

"How many exactly?" Tim responded.

Omar was clearly annoyed, but he took a breath and replied, "Ninety-four."

Tim continued, "Okay. And that's out of how many?"

Carol interjected, "One hundred and eighty-three."

Tim scrunched his eyebrows and tilted his head back. "That doesn't sound right." He turned to Barry for confirmation.

Carol interjected before Barry could clarify, "We have 587 TLCs across IUI, of which 183 are eligible for onboarding, and of which we have onboarded 94."

Barry jumped in. "I think what Tim is looking for is a breakdown of this. Maybe a chart that shows the TLCs that are considered in and out of scope for automated governance."

"Sure, we can break that down for you right now," Omar said, rising to the board.

"No, I need something I can share at the next huddle. I want to see a slide with, like, a box here," Tim said, gesturing above his head. "And then two boxes here . . ." He lowered his left hand and added in his right, signaling two boxes. "And then just keep stepping down with each one, explaining what's in what category and so on."

Omar and Michelle looked at each other and sheepishly nodded.

"We can do that," Michelle said as she turned her head toward Tim.

"Great, thanks." He stood up and started toward the exit.

The meeting had lasted only four minutes.

Barry hustled after Tim to chat on their way to the elevator. Carol, Omar, and Michelle stayed behind.

Omar waited until the door closed before lamenting his frustrations.

"What the heck was that?" he asked. "He didn't even want to hear us out. Why did Barry even call this meeting? And why do executives always need a slide deck?" Omar looked toward Carol, who lightly smiled but kept her eyes on her laptop as she checked her email inbox. She always tried to keep herself out of negative conversations.

Unsatisfied with Carol's passive response, Omar continued, "I mean, seriously! Tim didn't even want to talk through this, he only wanted to tell us how he wanted the slide to look. Doesn't that bother you?"

In his time at IUI, Omar had been used to engaging with leaders who always brought their whole self to a meeting. He was clearly irked by the short and dismissive tone that Tim struck.

"Yeah, it bothers me, but I get where he's coming from," Michelle replied. "Our pipelines are a mess, and that's a problem."

Michelle paused and took a deep breath before finally turning her attention away from her laptop screen toward Omar. "Last night I pulled every change record from the past year to cross-reference with our onboarding data. There are an additional twenty-two TLCs that we didn't account for in our initial data extraction."

"So now the total is 205?" Omar asked.

Michelle nodded.

"Wait, hang on, what does that mean? Those are all old apps, right?" Carol asked.

"Well, not necessarily," Michelle replied. "The twenty-two that I found are all relatively new applications . . ." She briefly paused. "At least based on our definitions."

"How were we missing them this whole time?" Carol asked, clearly upset at the apparent setback in their progress.

Michelle shrugged. "I don't know. But we're quickly running out of time."

Wednesday, January 4th

For the first time in her life, Michelle was starting to feel burned out. And it wasn't just the post-holiday blues. She was in bed with her laptop propped on a pillow. She had just finished the grueling task of getting her twins down for the night. She desperately wished she had some way of funneling a bit of their boundless energy. She could use it right now.

She felt like she had been endlessly squashing one obstacle after the next since the MRIA was first brought to IUI's attention more than nine months ago. And now, with the final deadline for delivering their engineering solution looming ever closer, they had been hit with yet another apparently unsolvable problem.

After three nights of combing through pipeline logs and code commits, Michelle felt herself losing sight of her original goal. She reached for her notepad and a pen, and wrote out an equation.

Total apps	205 (183 + 22 new)
Onboarded apps	− 94
Remaining	111

Legacy apps = ?
Remainder = ?

She felt much more comfortable after writing it down on paper. It didn't take her long to regain focus and dive back into the datasets.

She punched away at her keyboard as she wove an unholy web of messy, hard, duplicative Python code in her Jupyter notebook. As fervently as she espoused her beliefs of clean code when building software, she was quick to cut corners when it came to hacking scripts together to crunch data. But her sloppy scripting produced clean results, and that's all she needed at the moment. After another hour of aggregating data across disparate systems, she found a notable trend.

"Aha!"

"Shh." Her wife had just walked in. "You really want to wake the double tornado?"

"No! Sorry. But I think I finally figured something out."

"Excellent. Tell me all about it tomorrow. For now, you need to sleep." She reached across the bed and shut Michelle's laptop, lightly kissing her on the forehead.

Thursday, January 5th

The next day, Michelle joined the team late for standup. She had brought Carol with her. As they were getting closer and closer to the end date, they needed all the senior muscle they could get. When it was her turn, Michelle displayed her Jupyter notebook in a browser window. At first glance it looked like a confusing mixture of code and spreadsheets, layered vertically such that the user had to continuously scroll to see the resulting output.

As Michelle finished scrolling, she began to describe her findings.

"As you all know, we're now aware of 205 custom-developed IUI applications, of which we have onboarded 94. That means that we have 111 applications that remain unaccounted for. But after combing through our data, I found that at least three dozen of the 111 elusive applications shared similar idiosyncratic patterns across their code repositories."

"What do you mean?" asked Omar.

"Well, take this repository, for example: mortgage-account-migration-service," she pointed to the screen as she switched tabs to reveal the main page of the code repository, which displayed files and folders. "This code repository belongs to an application within the consumer lending division. Do you notice anything about the files in the root directory?" she asked.

"I don't see a build file," Omar added.

"Exactly!" said Michelle.

IUI used a tool for pipeline builds that required a specific type of build file in the root of the repository's directory to provide instructions to the build pipeline on how to test, compile, and publish the code in the repository. But the mortgage-account-migration-service repository did not have such a build file, and neither did any of the three dozen repositories that Michelle discovered the night before.

"How do they build their code if they don't have a build file?" asked Omar.

"I asked myself the same thing, but look at this file here . . ." Michelle slid her cursor over a file called "appfile.yaml" in the repository's root directory. She right-clicked and selected *Open Link in New Tab* from the list of options.

"See this?" she said as she gestured back toward the screen while the page loaded. "Each of the three dozen or so apps that I mentioned use this appfile.yaml."

"What the heck is that?" asked Omar.

"I wondered the same thing, but I called an old friend in the consumer lending division and they explained to me that a few years back they began building a framework called 'AppRails' that would abstract, standardize, and automate many of the nuanced configurations around consumer lending's CI/CD processes."

"Oh, I've heard of AppRails. They're such a pain to work with! Every time they have trouble deploying they come to us and say it's our fault," Dillon complained.

"Yep, that's the one," Michelle said with a slight smile.

"How did they get away with this one-off pipeline?" Omar asked.

"Well," Carol piped up. "It's not a one-off, it's legacy. Consumer lending is the newest division within IUI. When it comes to their technology, they're always starting fresh. The group was formed in the early days of DevOps and their leadership championed DevOps practices from the start, even before the rest of IUI began to onboard those practices. Thus, consumer lending built their own CI/CD process and automation outside of the emerging enterprise standards."

Omar interjected, "I still don't understand . . . what is AppRails?"

Michelle responded, "AppRails is the consumer lending pipeline."

"Well . . . it's more than that," Carol replied. "Yes, AppRails is the consumer lending build pipeline. But it also contains lots of 'black box' automation that handles things like dependency management and base images. They also use it to deploy. But the deployment part involves many manual approval steps—even though they make it look 'automated.'"

"How have they been allowed to do that for so long?" Omar asked.

Carol shrugged. "Back then there was no policy that mandated conforming to a single enterprise build and deploy pipeline, so they obtained admin service accounts to all of the tool chain platforms and servers, and they've been running their own CI/CD ever since."

"Michelle, what are we going to do?" Omar asked.

"I'm not sure," Michelle replied. How they were going to onboard a completely incompatible pipeline before their next meeting with Tim seemed an impossible mission.

"As much as I hate to admit failure, I don't think there's any way to get them onboarded in the time we have until the final completion date for remediation of the MRIA is here." Michelle turned to Carol.

Carol looked back at Michelle. "I think we'll have to get Jennifer involved."

"What have you got for me?" Jennifer said, getting straight to the point. It was late, and it was obvious she was eager to get through this meeting.

Carol had been able to get some time scheduled with Jennifer, the SVP of Engineering and CIO, at the end of the day for a brief fifteen-minute meeting. Michelle just hoped that would be enough time to convince her that Team Kraken had addressed enough of the MRIA's findings to move forward with the final report without onboarding every TLC, including the AppRails team. They would just need more time to finish the full transfer to the new system.

Carol started, "Well, as you know, Michelle and her team are working toward Tim's desire to achieve 100% onboarding of the new automated governance system before the project completion date with the regulators. But they've recently made a discovery that will certainly hinder that goal, if not derail it completely."

"Right. So as you know, we were hitting some great trajectory with onboarding using the automated onboarding at the 'checkout' stage for apps. But then it plateaued. We couldn't figure out why until we discovered that some of the apps weren't using our standard build files but were using . . ." Michelle paused. Jennifer looked like she was losing patience.

"Anyway, the point is that one of the consumer divisions is using AppRails, a completely different pipeline from the rest of IUI. There's just no way to get them onto Turbo Eureka before our deadline. We'll need at least a few months, if not more . . ."

"Hold on," Jennifer interrupted. "Why can't we just require them to make the switch? This is no time to be nice about it. Just get them onboard."

"Well, it's not quite that simple, Jennifer," Carol said.

"Enlighten me."

"Well, migrating the AppRails pipeline onto the enterprise pipeline will take a lot of money and time, and obviously we don't have the time at this moment. Even if we did, it's going to require a ton of hand holding . . ."

"If they can't migrate, then just combine the two pipelines. Smash them together or do whatever it is you need to do to make them compatible."

"It doesn't work that way. It's like having the wrong plug, Jennifer," Michelle interjected. "It's like you're trying to connect your phone's USB-C cable to your laptop but your laptop only has USB-A ports. And unlike in the real world, there is no converter out there. It's just not possible to smash the two systems together."

"So invent a converter and do it fast. We have to submit that final status report to Susan and the other execs next Tuesday. And we can't pass the external audit and the regulators with such a large number of important apps remaining outside the scope of onboarding for this automated governance solution. And . . ." Jennifer paused, took a deep breath, and said gravely, "If we don't pass, then I don't think I have to tell you that we'll all be on the job hunt. And good luck in the future with this failure on our heads."

Jennifer sat down, indicating an obvious end to the meeting. Carol and Michelle walked out and shut the door behind them.

"Shit," Michelle said, half under her breath. That had been no help at all.

Michelle left the office that day feeling defeated, to say the least. It was obvious that the stress of the looming deadline was putting everyone on edge. But Michelle had never been on a receiving end that bad before. It didn't seem like Carol had any sway here. They were going to have to find support from somewhere else. But where?

Over the next few weeks, Michelle and her team wracked their brains trying to come up with a solution. All the while they continued onboarding as many TLCs as they could.

The Friday before the "big meeting," as the team had come to call it, Michelle went home with a feeling of dread she hadn't experienced before. On Tuesday they would have to present their final MRIA response to the executive team. They would be showing how Turbo Eureka was addressing and solving every concern from the MRIA and the preceding MRAs before they took it to the CEO, then the board, and finally to the regulators. If the regulators weren't satisfied that IUI had mitigated the concerns from the MRAs and MRIAs, Michelle and her whole team, not to mention the rest of IUI, would be in serious trouble.

It was safe to say Michelle was feeling miserable. How were they going to convince everyone that they had accomplished enough in the last year to meet the MRIA findings? How could they convince everyone that 100% onboarding of the new system wasn't just unrealistic—it was simply impossible?

Michelle felt like a zombie as she sat through dinner that night. Later on she laid in her bed staring at the ceiling, listening to her wife's soft breathing. Most nights she would be asleep before her head hit the pillow, but not tonight. She could even hear the twins turning over in the other room. Her brain just couldn't shut off. There had to be some answer she hadn't thought of. Some silver bullet or golden ticket that would magically make everything fall neatly into place. In the early hours of the morning, she drifted off to sleep, but as she awoke, the sun just peeking through her blinds, her brain picked up where it had left off and whirred until the twins piled in, clamoring for cuddles.

All weekend, Michelle tried to forget about work and focus on her family. But she wasn't very successful. She found herself constantly sniping at her twins until her wife finally broke the tension by insisting on a movie marathon, complete with carpet picnic.

They watched some superhero flick, and Michelle actually cracked a smile watching her twins zooming around the room like characters from the movie, pretending to rescue their stuffed animals together. It was an unusual union, the two of them working together. More often than not they were like oil and water.

And she knew the feeling. It was like having to work with Audit: different points of view that never seem to mix. But sometimes, just like the success they had working with Bill, Barry, and Andrea, an unlikely union forms and you see the impossible become possible. Suddenly, an idea popped into Michelle's head. *Yes, that's it!* she thought with glee.

Monday, February 6th

Monday morning Michelle all but sprinted into the office and made her way straight to Andrea's desk. She wasn't in yet, so Michelle plopped herself down in Andrea's chair, bouncing her leg with impatience. There was a framed picture of Andrea on her desk, her back to the camera, but her piles of red hair cascading down her back were unmistakable. She was on top of a mountain, looking up at the Milky Way. A blonde dog sat next to her. Next to the picture, an empty South Park coaster sat and a cute pink and white striped jar of candy grabbed Michelle's attention. Michelle couldn't help herself. She lifted the lid and had just stuck her fingers in when she heard someone.

"Help yourself."

"Oh, sorry!" Michelle spun around, dropping the lid back on the jar a bit more forcefully than she meant to. Andrea laughed. "Sorry. Um, good morning. I have a request of you—well, of Audit, I meant." Michelle stood up, offering Andrea her seat.

"Okay. You have a request of Audit? Go ahead," Andrea said, sitting down in her chair and looking at Michelle with an air of curiosity.

Michelle launched into the same explanation she had given Jennifer, keeping it as succinct as she could, pacing herself as she saw that Andrea was actively and thoughtfully listening. "So, I've come here looking for some support from Audit. If Audit could back us up, if they could show that we've made a good-faith effort and that we have plans to onboard the rest of the TLCs, but that we just need more time, then we might all make it through the Big Meeting with our jobs still intact."

"Why can't these teams using AppRails be merged?" Andrea asked.

"They can be, but it will take more time than we have," Michelle tried to explain.

"Okay, now let's walk this back," Andrea said. "AppRails can't be migrated in time to meet the deadline. But that 100% onboarding deadline was set by Tim, right? But tomorrow's meeting is all about showing that we've delivered on our promises to the regulators. All we need to do is ensure that our response has specifically addressed the concerns in the MRIA to be compliant. So what was the exact language from the MRIA again?"

"You're right! Wait a second. Let me pull that up." Michelle opened her laptop, glad she came straight to Andrea's desk before dropping her stuff off at her own. "Here it is. The MRIA said they found 'inconsistent process, ineffective in ensuring security and compliance, resulting in unauthorized and vulnerable software with a significant number of defects being released to production.'"

Andrea read the line over and over again. Michelle just stared at her, impatient but trying to give her the time she needed to figure out a solution.

"I need coffee," Andrea blurted out. Michelle gaped at her as Andrea walked off and came back a few minutes later with a steaming mug in her hands. She sat back down and looked at the MRIA findings again.

"So," Michelle prodded.

"Shh," was Andrea's only response.

Michelle slumped onto the floor, her back against Andrea's cubicle wall. Just as she thought she was about to nod off, Andrea broke the silence.

"Aha!" Andrea said, with a bit too much enthusiasm. "Sorry, but this is perfect. It's so simple. You have your answer right there."

"I do? But we haven't got all the TLCs onboard with our automated governance, and we won't be able to before the deadline. Tim is adamant that we need 100% . . ."

"Tell me, dear Watson," Andrea said, a small smirk forming on her face. "Where in the MRIA does it say the word 'automated?'"

Michelle chewed on that for a moment. "Well, uh, it doesn't."

"Exactly. Based on the language in the MRIA, I think we're satisfactorily meeting the requirements as long as every TLC at IUI is following the same set of rules that we laid out, which are:

- Enforce peer reviews of code that is pushed to a production environment.
- Identify and enforce minimum quality gates.
- Remove all elevated access to all production environments for everyone.

The MRIA doesn't give us any specifications about how to follow those rules. Turbo Eureka has solved this for most of the TLCs for the enterprise that are using enterprise standard. It's on AppRails pipeline users to provide evidence of these for every production release from now onwards," Andrea explained.

"So, as is, AppRails deployment has manual processes involving multiple approval steps," Michelle replied. "But it's not going to be easy for them with this extra manual work, and they may not have a system to store the evidence."

"Well, AppRails and other teams will have to manually upload the evidence to the CMDB system. They need to review those with the CAB and get their approval captured before they release anything." Andrea sounded like she wanted to make things harder for teams that weren't willing to onboard onto automated governance. "And we'll audit them frequently to make sure they are following all the policies laid out in the automated version."

"Seriously? 'Cause I just don't think that's going to fly with Tim and Jennifer."

"Well, let's get some more muscle to back us up." Andrea winked. "And by the way, between you and me, I hope this manual work causes some extra pain to the AppRails users. It may actually push them to migrate to the enterprise standards sooner."

Andrea turned to her computer and began typing a message into the interoffice chat. "I'll see if we can't get on Jada's calendar before the end of the day. She's usually good about keeping a few ten-minute spots on her calendar open for unexpected asks from her team."

"Do you really think it's this easy? That we've actually fulfilled the requirements?"

"You know, Audit isn't out to make your lives difficult. We're actually here to help," Andrea said with a smile. "So, yeah. As long as these other teams are manually following the policies laid out in the automated governance, then we've achieved our goal. We are doing what we say we are doing."

Michelle smiled back. It felt good to have Audit on her team instead of feeling like they were against her. In fact, she finally felt like they were really fulfilling on all the promises made by DevOps in the first place. There didn't need to be walls between silos. Audit didn't need to be the enemy, the oil to their water. They really could work together. And it felt great when they did.

CHAPTER 13

Tuesday, February 7th

Carol and Michelle walked into the conference room. All the bosses, and the bosses of the bosses, were there, including one of the representatives from the external audit firm, Laura Perez. Even Jason was in attendance. Tim and Jada were sitting in the front two seats of the table, right across from each other. Tim's back was facing the windows. It was a nice day out. Bright, sunny, and not a cloud in the sky. But inside Michelle could have sworn she saw a storm gathering overhead. This meeting was going to be anything but smooth sailing.

Michelle set her things down and tried to look calm. She scanned the table, noticing Jennifer next to Tim. Jason had spun his chair around as soon as he heard them walk in.

"Well, the stars of our show!" Jason said excitedly, briefly clapping his hands.

As his clapping settled down, Jada stood up.

"Not that we need a reminder, but let's start with why we are here today. Nearly one year ago, we got served with an MRIA from regulators for, and I quote," Jada read off the paper in front of her, "*Inconsistent process, ineffective in ensuring security and compliance, resulting in unauthorized and vulnerable software with significant amount of defects being released to production.*"

"Over the last ten months and change, since we were first hit with the MRIA, we have made a lot of advancements. And we've made a lot of mistakes. But today, IUI is barreling down a new path to delivering software in a way that includes everyone who has a concern with the software we write internally."

Jason clapped again. Michelle looked at him—clearly he wasn't feeling the same stress as she was. What did he know that she didn't?

"What we will walk you through next is the core of our strategy to resolve these findings and prevent—er, significantly reduce the likelihood of similar future findings. With that, I'm going to turn it over to Bill, who's been working with a team of engineers, Security, and Audit to craft our response and the future of governance here at IUI."

Bill stood up. Michelle swallowed. She, Omar, and the whole team had been working for so long on this project that she felt like she was watching her own child stand up to present their PhD dissertation. She begged the butterflies in her stomach to settle down.

"We're not here today because we failed an audit or were hit with an MRIA; we are here today because we failed to think bigger and better about how we build software," Bill said. "In retrospect, we did a lot of things right as we transitioned to a DevOps way of working, but we didn't do all the right things. That's why our software engineering process failed us: we only considered Development and Operations, Dev and Ops, not Security, Compliance, or Risk. This was our big failing."

Once again, Jason clapped briefly, nodding his head in agreement.

"Our problem was that we did not have proper controls in our software development process, hence all the MRAs leading up to the MRIA. How did we not catch this? These findings could have been preempted if software engineering had engaged our Risk teams in order to build out our software delivery workflows to include the proper controls. Why did we not do this? Well, simply put, it was not how we thought about DevOps. We thought speed of delivery trumped everything else. We failed to include security and risk as features of our product. This lack of early inclusion and continued cooperation leads us to the primary issue.

"I am now convinced that this primary issue was a misguided perspective for assessing what the requirements of our software development and delivery process should have been," Bill explained.

Jada commented, " I think we all have a bit of a misguided perspective there too. We've talked about more cooperation with the Engineering teams, although we've been at a loss on how to make that happen. Being explicit partners and contributors to the design of the software development process is a great approach."

Another series of small golf claps could be heard from Jason.

"Yes, well said," Jason chimed in. "This is an example of the three ways of DevOps: flow, feedback, and continuous improvement. This type of collaboration between teams establishes flow, and flow is about ensuring that defects are not passed to the end user. We can look at risk and compliance with either the software delivery process or the software itself as a quality validation. This is a profound understanding of how the IUI 'system,' and I say that broadly speaking, could work."

Everyone at the table now had a light smile.

Michelle smiled. *Wow. Are we actually learning and growing together? Maybe this won't be such a bad meeting after all . . .*

"Okay, on to our guiding policies," Bill started. "Think of these as the guardrails. A guiding policy does not tell you the actions you must take. Instead, they give you the right amount of information to choose the actions you should consider to solve the problem. They channel the action into a specific direction without explicitly stating what should be done. First guiding policy: if the rest of these policies are abided by, then you can bypass the IUI manual change approval process and go straight to production."

With those words, you could practically hear the proverbial record scratch. Jada and Tim's faces went from excited to concerned. This proposal had been in front of them in the past, but neither of them wanted to touch the topic. They had heard it from the developers earlier; now they were hearing the same from product management. But more than one IUI team members' careers had focused on the manual change approval process. The CAB was at the center of every change that went into production. Everyone dreaded going in front of the CAB and presenting a change request form. The notion of skipping the IUI change approval process was very disruptive.

"Jada, Tim, your faces say it all. But think of it like TSA Pre-Check: less risky passengers get to move through the process faster. Let me finish real quick, and then we can talk about your concerns. I bet we'll address them with these other three policies."

Both Jada and Tim looked at each other, then at Bill, signaling permission to move forward.

Bill glanced at the slides and continued. "Second guiding policy: complete automation must be implemented for capturing evidence of quality, risk mitigation, and compliance for software and its delivery process. The only manual process is peer review, which is a must when software is being designed and developed.

"Third guiding policy: security and compliance requirements are as important as functional requirements, and hence all software product teams must involve Security, Risk, Compliance, and Audit teams to identify these requirements from day one.

"Fourth guiding policy: the software budget. A budgeting system, similar to a financial budget, will be established to track our deficit in quality, risk, compliance, and audit. When a budget has been exhausted, the team cannot work any new features and must pay down the debt completely. This budget shall be available for anyone in the company to see at any time," Bill said before taking a deep breath. It seemed like the first one he'd taken since he'd begun.

"Wait, why won't every team be 100% compliant all the time? Why would we ever want to allow anything less than 100%?" Tim continued, "Gee . . . don't we already know why we are here?"

Carol replied, "While we want to always achieve 100% compliance with any rule we set out for the organization, the reality is that that's largely unachievable. When we set our rules, we have no feedback process for how arduous it is to achieve them; the organization just assumes they will be met because 'it's the edict.'

"In practice it's quite the opposite. Most will try to meet the expectation, although when a conflict comes up that pulls them in another direction, many will rationalize their work as 'good enough.' We can't really empirically track what is and isn't in compliance with rules.

"Taking this new approach acknowledges risk and provides a mitigating framework for addressing it empirically. The product teams will be empowered to make the trade-off decisions since they have the most context. Leadership, such as yourself, can set the specific budget limits. This now makes quality, risk, compliance, security, and audit the responsibility of the product team."

"So you are saying that we could release a new version of a software with a known critical vulnerability? And we will allow product teams to make that decision?" Tim asked.

Jason quickly interrupted with a small whoop. "Security is the responsibility of the engineering team! Decision-making is closest to those with the most context! Yes! Congratulations, Carol; you sound a lot like Shannon Lietz. I think she was one of those who coined the term 'DevSecOps.' Her foundational idea was to make security the responsibility of those who are actually building the software, not some other folks who have little knowledge of the software and business problem. It's the epitome of bringing the authority to information, not the other way around."

Michelle had been trying to interject for a while, and finally she was able to get a word in edgewise. "I can give you some examples. Let's look at two examples of compliance policies: policy number one, 'no software releases are allowed with a known critical vulnerability,' and policy number two, 'unit test code coverage for new code must be at least 60% for a new release.' I can confidently say that no one would release critically vulnerable code to production, but the team may decide to move ahead with, say, 55% code coverage and commit to bring it up during the future releases. No matter what the teams do, we will have the evidence of what they did, and I think that is what we were lacking before all this."

"Okay, this is compelling. I need to get a bit more comfortable with the idea, but I see where you all are coming from," Tim said.

Jason turned to Tim. "What the team is proposing has similar fundamental concepts to those that underpin SRE.[1] Where SRE is focused on enhancing the software, or software development process, for reliability and for end users, this fourth policy is enhancing the software and development process for compliance and security. Heck, if we do this right, we may be able to write a Compliance and Security Engineering book like Google did when they published the SRE book!" Jason looked positively giddy. Not for the first time, Michelle wondered where his source of unending positivity came from.

---

1. SRE (site reliability engineering) adopts software engineering principles and practices and applies them to infrastructure and operations problems. The main goal is to create highly reliable and scalable software systems. See https://sre.google/.

"The CSE book!" Tim smirked.

Another click was heard and the second-to-last slide of the presentation appeared: "Next Steps."

Bill looked at Michelle, Carol, Barry, and Andrea.

"We'll take it from here," Michelle said. "The following is the dashboard we will be working with."

On the screen were the words, "Why would we not want this?" The slide featured a dashboard that broke down pull request approval, unit test code coverage, static code quality, and more.

"But wait, there's more," Michelle continued. "Look at how we now view our system down to the component level." She advanced to the next slide.

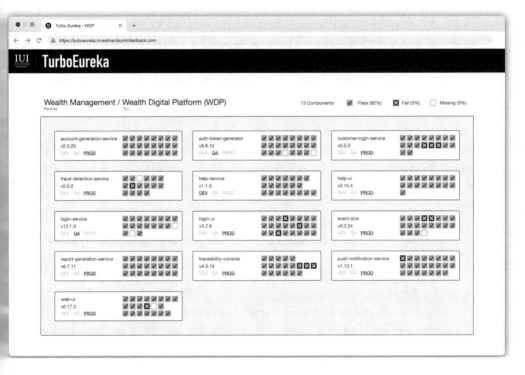

"I want this," Jennifer said.

Not even a tenth of a second passed before the external auditor, Laura Perez, said, "Wow! Yes, me too. I don't think I've ever seen something quite like this before. In fact, I'd be very eager to talk with your team more about how we might use this example to help other organizations achieve this. Maybe even present a joint experience report at a conference or something."

Michelle beamed. She couldn't wait to tell Omar and the rest of Team Kraken how well their work was being received.

All eyes turned to Jada. She was still in deep thought. Her five-second pause felt like five minutes. It then became clear that Jada was awestruck.

"Yes, I want this! I want this, like, yesterday. Let's face it: we've told ourselves that we've had a plan for reducing risk in DevOps forever. But at best . . . at best we've had three different plans: one in our Engineering teams, another plan from our Cyber Risk folks, and another from Internal Audit. Now, for the first time, automated governance will ensure all three functions will all be aligned to the same vision of what it means to reduce risk as we build software for the business."

Tim nodded. "Yes, this looks better than the last demo I saw. I think it's clear to say that what your team has built is a game changer, not just for IUI but for the community at large. But let's talk about onboarding. How many teams are now using this at IUI?"

Michelle's stomach flip-flopped. This was the moment she was dreading. She pulled up another screen, which showed a step-down ladder of the TLCs at IUI. Michelle walked everyone through the onboarding process to date, including how they had used the "checkout" stage in the pipeline to automate onboarding before they discovered the plateau in adoptions and the AppRails platform.

Michelle steeled herself. "With the discovery of this legacy platform, we've essentially hit a roadblock." Michelle avoided Tim's eyes and went on. "We're proposing dedicating the necessary time and budget over the next quarter, at least, to helping them onboard. In addition, there are other legacy apps that will be too costly to try and migrate over. Instead, we are proposing maintaining a manual process for these . . ."

Michelle trailed off as murmurs and comments began flying around the room.

"What good is this new automated system if half the organization doesn't follow it?" Tim said.

"This isn't going to go over well with the regulators. Once again, we're not meeting our burden of security," Barry said.

"I agree. Susan and the board aren't going to like this," Jennifer said.

At that moment, just as it looked like the meeting was going to dissolve into another blame game, Jada stood up.

"Everyone calm down. Now, Michelle and her team have achieved an amazing amount in the last year. Let's not overlook the enthusiasm you were all just showing minutes ago when she displayed the new dashboards."

"Yes, the dashboards are great. But it doesn't do us any good if they're not being used," Tim said, obviously exasperated. He turned to Jada. "Do we think we can move forward with anything less than 100% onboarding? I'm not sure."

Michelle felt her cheeks turn red. She simultaneously felt ashamed and frustrated, a feat she didn't know was possible.

"One hundred percent onboarding is just not feasible," Michelle responded. "And it's even irresponsible in some cases. Some of the legacy apps would spend more time and money trying to force their square peg into our round hole than if they just keep doing what they're doing. Better to let them live out their days comfortably achieving manual compliance until it's time to sunset them."

"But that's putting IUI at risk of even more audits and another MRIA!"

"Actually, I don't think it is," Jada responded. "Michelle and her team brought their concerns around onboarding to Audit so we could work this problem together." Jada turned to Michelle and Andrea and smiled. "And rightly so. As we dug into the problem, we went back to the original findings of the MRIA and our own internal audits.

"Now, if you'll remember, the MRIA states that IUI was found to have 'inconsistent process, ineffective in ensuring security and compliance, resulting in unauthorized and vulnerable software with significant amount of defects being released to production.' Nowhere in this audit do regulators state *how* we are to correct this. There's no requirement to onboard every app at IUI onto an automated governance system. As long as everyone at IUI is doing what they say they're doing, and we have the evidence of that, we're in compliance."

"Automated governance was our choice and probably the only way out to continue on our DevOps journey," Michelle added.

"What about the original TLCs called out in the previous MRAs?" Laura interjected. "Are they on this new automated system?"

"The majority are, yes," Michelle answered. "All except the TLCs on the AppRails platform. But those are following the manual policies we've put in place and spoke about at the beginning of the meeting."

There was silence in the room. Everyone felt a little uneasy having this discussion in the presence of an external auditor. Michelle wasn't quite sure if she felt like standing up and cheering at how far they'd come, or slumping in her chair as she thought about a year of work and what some might think is very little to show.

All eyes turned to Laura from the external auditor firm. Ultimately, the board was most likely to agree and follow whatever she and her firm said.

"Mmm hmm," Laura responded, nodding her head. "I think Jada is correct. The MRIA doesn't require *how* IUI addresses the concerns, just that the concerns are effectively addressed. Whether some sections of the organization are in compliance manually or through the automated system shouldn't make a difference. I think that with what you've put in place here, and with a clear plan for migrating or addressing these controls in the future, you should be able to convince the regulators and close out this project. Remember, the regulators' biggest concern is that you show you are actively reducing risk."

Michelle held her breath, looking around the room. Tim had leaned back in his chair and was staring at Laura. Jennifer had her head cocked in an appraising way. There was silence for what felt like an eternity.

Then Michelle was startled to once again hear clapping. She turned to the back of the room. Jason was now standing and clapping loudly. The rest of the room had turned to face him, many with quizzical looks on their faces.

"Congratulations! You've done it," Jason announced.

"Done it?" Tim said.

"Yes! I'm convinced. And so is Laura, I take it." He turned to her and everyone could see her nodding in agreement. Jason continued in a calm voice, "Look, nearly a year ago, IUI almost came to a full stop, and its future existence came into question. Susan had only two choices: to give up or to trust her team. She picked the second. It was unfortunate that it had to come down to that. It didn't need to be that way!"

Everyone was looking at Jason's face. Tim wasn't sure what to expect.

"Just like all other companies, we embarked on a DevOps journey over the last few years. Just like all other companies, we started embracing the goodness of DevOps across our teams. The leadership was proud of what was going on. And then the MRIA shook our world.

"We had all the right people in the right places. They just needed to come together to create the magic. That should have been simple, right? But it wasn't. Teams didn't come together. We eventually ended up in a place where we even questioned our own existence or ability to survive.

"Over the last year, everyone in this organization felt the pain, yet they went above and beyond. I applaud our engineering teams that looked outside the box. They didn't shy away from experimenting, testing out innovative solutions, and even failing multiple times. But they did not give up!" Jason looked at Jennifer, Carol, and Michelle and clapped once more. "We even had one of the worst supply chain vulnerabilities hit us during this process, and this team took care of that too!

"To our Risk and Audit partners . . . thank you! Thank you!" Jason was genuinely appreciative of how Jada and her team stood up to the cause. "Tim and his team also supported us during all this. So, thank you, Tim, and everyone from your team as well.

"Finally, I've been thinking about this for a few days now. I'm asking myself if we are way better off now when it comes to software development security, audit, and risk management." Jason paused for a moment, looked around, and continued. "I am now convinced that if we aren't using DevOps principles to embrace continuous integration and continuous delivery practices, we aren't going to be compliant enough. "

Jason paused, smiled broadly, and looked around the room once again. "I am so proud to be part of this team. You should all be proud too! I believe we just marked an indelible turning point for IUI. And you and your teams made this happen! What do you think, Jada? "

"I agree! Well put, Jason," Jada replied. "Very well put. Great job, team!"

Jason began clapping again and everyone joined in. Michelle smiled and felt goosebumps. She looked at Carol, Bill, Tim, Jada, and others in the room. They were all smiling. Even Barry had managed to muster a grin as he joined in on the applause. *Incredible!* Michelle thought to herself. *We actually did it.*

As the clapping began to subside, Jada concluded, "Now, unless there are any other concerns, I think we can adjourn." Jada paused to look around the room.

Laura gave a shake of her head. "I have no objections."

"Excellent," Tim said. "I think we're ready to present our new processes and procedures to the board. Carol, Michelle, you and your team should continue your work onboarding TLCs. We may have pushed obstacles off our path and paved a road for the future, but that road needs constant maintenance. Our next step is going to be ensuring IUI is never put in this situation again."

"Hear, hear," Jason said. "Well, if you'll excuse me, I'll just go and fill Susan in on the great work you all have done."

Jason left the room and the other execs began gathering their things. Michelle picked her things up as well. She couldn't quite believe they had made it through.

"Thanks, Jason," Susan said grinning from ear to ear.

Jason had just updated her on the progress and was joined by several from the leadership team.

"I'm incredibly proud of what the team was able to accomplish," Susan continued. "And, this Michelle, she seems like someone we would want to invest in."

"Absolutely!" Jason exclaimed, adding, "Jennifer's team did a great job but Michelle was the Sherpa that got us over the mountain."

"I agree completely, she's definitively a leader we need to promote," Jennifer added.

"She even impressed me," Jada said, "and that's not easy to do."

Jason laughed and stood to leave, "We should make sure Michelle gets the recognition she deserves. Heck, the whole team should be recognized! I suggest Jada and Tim kick it off with a karaoke party. I hear you two are hidden stars!"

Jada's mouth dropped open. "How did you know?"

"Don't worry, I won't bring witnesses," Jason said.

Everyone laughed

EPILOGUE

Tuesday, March 4th

Susan was sitting at her desk, reading through the latest book Jason had given her to read, when her phone buzzed. She picked it up and saw that it was Bernard.

"Susan," Bernard's voice rang from the other end as she answered. "Just heard back from the examiner. Looks like your team pulled it off."

"That's excellent news, Bernard!"

"This is great work. The whole board is feeling confident."

"Thank you. I'll pass that news on to the whole team. Have a great weekend."

"You as well."

Bernard hung up, and Susan placed her phone back on the desk. She packed up her laptop, the book from Jason, and various print-outs of papers and articles Jason had sent her, all on the future of technology businesses.

She walked out the front doors of IUI. *I just love Boston in the spring*, she thought to herself as she made her way past the towering buildings. She glanced over to drink in the view of the Charles River Esplanade. The air was crisp and cool but soon the trees would be budding and painting the glassy river with a brilliant green glow. She smiled. It reminded her of all the reasons she had relocated to this area in the first place.

There was construction in front of the neighboring building. Large water pipes, power conduits, and steel reinforcing bars were all exposed. Susan thought to herself how soon it would all disappear, and in its place, a pleasing landscape and facade would emerge. It struck her, reflecting back on all that had happened at IUI, that technology and security are like those buried elements. When done well, they can't be seen from the outside. They're invisible to the customer and even to the company itself. But if they're not included in the business strategy and execution, then the business would be missing critical flow, power, and structure to make it all work. Things may appear to be going well, but just under the surface there would be problems.

She took a deep breath, feeling the weight of her briefcase filled with books, articles, and papers. If anyone had told her two decades ago that as a CEO she would need to become an expert in technology and security, she would have laughed. Sure, technology and security are important but they're like utilities, cost centers in service to the business. Leave it to the smart nerds and paranoids in the basement. Right?

She realized now how misguided that thinking was. As Jason had reminded her, not only is technology the lifeblood of the business, it is key to amplifying and accelerating everything they do. By keeping it at arm's length, they had inadvertently allowed it to lose connection with the business. Security, audit, and process gaps formed and had been amplified. However beautiful their shiny business might be on the outside, cracks had formed, and they suddenly found themselves hurtling toward disaster.

A cool blast of air hit Susan as she rounded the corner. She looked up and saw dark clouds starting to gather in the sky. City noise filled the air and washed up against the office buildings as business travelers made their way home from work. *There is always a buzz and energy in the air here*, Susan thought to herself. She wondered how many of her fellow travelers were likely to face the same challenges she and IUI had just gone through, and how many more challenges waited in IUI's future.

The street was lined with office buildings. Each one seemed to try to stretch just slightly taller than its neighbor. Capturing business in this competitive landscape demanded innovation, speed, relevance, and security. Each layer of technology was like a floor in the buildings that Susan saw in front of her. Every layer prepared the foundation for the next, and the next, all the way into the future. For IUI or any business like it to survive and thrive, no separation can be allowed between the business and the technology that powers and builds it. She was convinced that now, more than ever, every business was truly a technology business and every business leader was a technology leader.

After speaking with Jason earlier in the day, her head was full of new ideas for IUI to try. All of them powered by new digital technologies. She felt a surge of excitement as she thought of all the possibilities. Anxiety tapped her shoulder, but she brushed it off. After all, she had the best team in the world. Sure, they would make mistakes, but as they had just experienced, she was convinced that they would be able to tackle any challenge if they worked together.

The sky's the limit! She thought to herself, looking at the towering buildings in front of her. *No, on second thought, there is no limit. We just need to have the courage to pursue it. Our future is truly unlimited!*

Susan laughed. She was ready to change the world. But not tonight. Tonight, well, tonight was pizza night. She couldn't wait to get home to Rich and Lucas and start building some of those pizza pies.

MRAs AND MRIAs

MRAs are deficiencies that are important and should be addressed over a reasonable period of time, but where the institution's response need not be immediate. No matter how serious the concern, it is addressed to the institution's board of directors.

MRAs describe practices that:

1. Deviate from sound governance, internal control, or risk-management principles, and have the potential to adversely affect the bank's condition, including its financial performance or risk profile, if not addressed.
2. Result in substantive noncompliance with laws or regulations, enforcement actions, or conditions imposed in writing in connection with the approval of any application or other request by the bank.

The Office of the Comptroller of the Currency (OCC) refers to such practices as deficient practices. Such practices also may be unsafe or unsound generally, any action, or lack of action that is contrary to generally accepted standards of prudent operation and the possible consequences of which, if continued, would be abnormal risk or loss or damage to an institution, its shareholders, or the Deposit Insurance Fund.

MRIAs arise from an examination, inspection, or any other supervisory activity and are matters of significant importance and urgency that the Federal Reserve requires banking organizations to address immediately and include:

1. matters that have the potential to pose significant risk to the safety and soundness of the banking organization,
2. matters that represent significant noncompliance with applicable laws or regulations,
3. repeat criticisms that have escalated in importance due to insufficient attention or inaction by the banking organization,
4. and, in the case of consumer compliance examinations, matters that have the potential to cause significant consumer harm. An MRIA will remain an open issue until resolution and examiners confirm the banking organization's corrective actions.

5. For more, see the following references:

https://www.federalreserve.gov/supervisionreg/srletters/sr1313a1.pdf

https://www.federalregister.gov/documents/2017/08/09/2017-16735/proposed-guidance-on-supervisory-expectation-for-boards-of-directors

https://www.occ.gov/publications-and-resources/publications/comptrollers-handbook/files/bank-supervision-process/pub-ch-bank-supervision-process.pdf (pg 51)

PIPELINE DESIGN WITH CONTROL TOLLGATES

An organization might design their pipelines using a concept of "controls and toll-gates." The idea is that certain types of gates in the pipeline can be used to alert or stop the software delivery process. Here are examples of sixteen such controls/tollgates:

- source code version control
- optimum branching strategy
- static analysis
- >80% code coverage
- vulnerability scan
- open-source scan
- artifact version control
- automated provisioning
- immutable servers
- integration testing
- performance testing
- build deploy testing automated for every commit
- automated rollback
- automated change order
- zero downtime release
- feature toggle

Controls in the Build Pipeline
Many events in a build pipeline can be collected and saved in a tamper proof format. Once available, they may:

- inform decisions to block a build
- trigger alerts monitored by a security operations team
- serve as attestation that controls were performed prior to deployment

As more controls from across the software development life cycle are implemented and their events are securely collected in a single place, the likelihood of risky software in production decreases, IT leaders and regulators will have improved visibility that inspires trust, and the organization enjoys safer software that allows it to accomplish its mission.

This table offers a few options readers may consider implementing in their own build pipelines. A list of more than thirty controls you may consider storing can be found on page 34 of the IT Revolution white paper *DevOps Automated Governance Reference Architecture.*

Control #	Control	Included in the IUI story?	Might you use this to block a build?
1	Peer Review	Yes	Yes; lack of peer review may block a build.
2	Static Application Security Testing	Yes	Yes; critical and (optionally) high findings may block a build.
3	Software Composition Analysis	Yes	Yes; critical and (optionally) high findings may block a build.
4	Code Quality	Yes	Probably not.
5	Unit Testing	Yes	Probably not.
6	Code Signing	Yes	Yes; lack of code signing may block a build.
7	License Check	No	Probably not.
8	Trusted Dependency Store	No	Yes; use of dependencies originating outside the trusted store may block a build.
9	Container Vulnerability Scan	No	Yes; critical and (optionally) high findings may block a build.
10	Secrets Scanning	No	Yes; the presence of sensitive tokens, keys, passwords, etc. in the source code may block a build.

DEVSECOPS MANIFESTO

Through security as code, we have and will learn that there is simply a better way for security practitioners, like us, to operate and contribute value with less friction. We know we must adapt our ways quickly and foster innovation to ensure data security and privacy issues are not left behind because we were too slow to change.

By developing security as code, we will strive to create awesome products and services, provide insights directly to developers, and generally favor iteration over trying to always come up with the best answer before a deployment. We will operate like developers to make security and compliance available to be consumed as services. We will unlock and unblock new paths to help others see their ideas become a reality.

We won't simply rely on scanners and reports to make code better. We will attack products and services like an outsider to help you defend what you've created. We will learn the loopholes, look for weaknesses, and work with you to provide remediation actions instead of long lists of problems for you to solve on your own.

We will not wait for our organizations to fall victim to mistakes and attackers. We will not settle for finding what is already known; instead, we will look for anomalies yet to be detected. We will strive to be a better partner by valuing what you value:

- Leaning in over always saying "No"
- Data and security science over fear, uncertainty, and doubt
- Open contribution and collaboration over security-only requirements
- Consumable security services with APIs over mandated security controls and paperwork
- Business-driven security scores over rubber-stamp security
- Red and Blue Team exploit testing over relying on scans and theoretical vulnerabilities
- 24/7 proactive security monitoring over reacting after being informed of an incident
- Shared threat intelligence over keeping info to ourselves
- Compliance operations over clipboards and checklists

You can read the full DevSecOps manifesto here: https://www.devsecops.org/

SHIFT LEFT

As with most things related to DevOps and DevSecOps, the term "shift left" can be traced all the way back to Toyota Production Systems and the use of the Jidoka and the Andon Cord. The main idea is that when delivering products, it's more cost effective to find defects earlier in the process. This leads to higher-quality output, as well. The first use of "shift left" in software delivery can be traced back to software testing in the software development life cycle (SDLC).

Shift-left testing is important because it helps to prevent the following types of harm due to late testing:

- Testers may be less involved in initial planning, often resulting in insufficient resources being allocated to testing.
- Defects in requirements, architecture, and design remain undiscovered while significant effort is wasted implementing them.
- Debugging (including identifying, localizing, fixing, and regression-testing defects) becomes harder as more software is produced and integrated.
- Encapsulation impedes white-box testing, reducing code coverage during testing.
- There is less time to fix defects found by testing, thereby increasing the likelihood that they will be postponed until later increments or versions of the system. This creates a "bow wave" of technical debt that can sink projects if it grows too large.[1]

The agile movement promoted Test-Driven Development (TDD) as a "shift-left" concept. It was the DevOps movement that really formalized the idea of "shift left" as a common term. Gene Kim et al. further explored this concept of "shift left"

---

1. Wikipedia, "Shift-Left Testing," modified November 8, 2021. https://en.wikipedia.org/wiki/Shift-left _testing#:~:text=Defects%20in%20requirements%2C%20architecture%2C%20and,software%20is %20produced%20and%20integrated.

in the book *The DevOps Handbook*. In it, they describes the Second Way as a process of amplifying feedback loops.

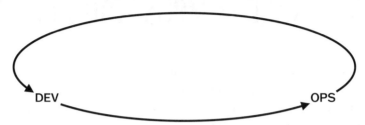

In 2014, Andrew Storms tied the concept of "shift left" to security in an article for DevOps.com called "Moving Security to the Left in a DevOps World."

A concise summary of "shifting left" may be the intentional prioritization of controls, behaviors, and capabilities in the SDLC that prevent defects in software in production rather than those which detect and respond to such defects.

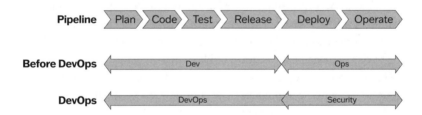

SOFTWARE COMPOSITION ANALYSIS

Software Composition Analysis (SCA) is the process of identifying the components that comprise a given piece of software. The components may be identified at a range of levels, from higher level (such as corresponding to items in "cloud diagrams") to mid level (such as distinct classes, modules, or files) to low level (such as functions or methods comprising a file or class).

The software to be examined may be generally perceived as a single monolithic entity (in which case SCA aims to reveal its constituent components), or it may—as in the case of modern operating systems—already be seen as a collection of components (in which case SCA may identify components at a greater level of granularity or identify the interrelationships among already-known components).

The term SCA may also refer to the analysis of a single component, showing for example its inputs, outputs, and side effects.

In the industry, SCA is often viewed as limited to identification of open source used within a software product. For example, a typical definition is: "SCA is the process of automating visibility into the use of open source software (OSS) for the purpose of risk management, security, and license compliance." However, SCA does not need to be limited to open-source and may include identification of proprietary third-party or in-house components. The common restriction to open source may be based on if software components are invisible without source code. However, software reverse-engineering, including both static examination (e.g., disassembly and decompilation) and dynamic examination (e.g., packet sniffing) of commercial products, provides often-feasible methods to determine the composition of software without the benefit of source code.

The purposes of SCA include security audits (particularly when a product's use of a particular version of a component can be identified and compared to repositories of known security vulnerabilities), license compliance (both OSS and proprietary components), and intellectual property infringement.

The SCA process should produce a valid software bill of materials (SBOM) or a "software tear down." The industry is aligning on the CycloneDX and SPDX standard formats for SBOMs.

US EXECUTIVE ORDER ON IMPROVING THE NATION'S CYBERSECURITY

On May 12, 2021, President Biden signed an executive order to improve the nation's cybersecurity and to protect federal government networks. This executive order was directly related to recent cybersecurity incidents such as SolarWinds, Microsoft Exchange, and the Colonial Pipeline.

"It is the policy of my administration that the prevention, detection, assessment, and remediation of cyber incidents is a top priority and essential to national and economic security. The federal government must lead by example. All federal information systems should meet or exceed the standards and requirements for cybersecurity set forth in and issued pursuant to this order."[1]

In short, the executive order calls for the:[2]

- Removal of barriers to threat information sharing between government and the private sector.
- Modernizing and implementing stronger cybersecurity standards in the federal government.
- Improving software supply chain security.
- Establishing a Cybersecurity Safety Review Board.
- Creating a standard playbook for responding to cyber incidents.
- Improving detection of cybersecurity incidents on federal government networks.
- Improving investigative and remediation capabilities.

1. https://www.whitehouse.gov/briefing-room/presidential-actions/2021/05/12/executive-order-on-improving-the-nations-cybersecurity/
2. https://www.whitehouse.gov/briefing-room/presidential-actions/2021/05/12/executive-order-on-improving-the-nations-cybersecurity/

FAQ

This section is meant to provide general guidance on how to think about embarking on an automated governance effort and dispel misconceptions that may inhibit readers from getting started.

1. **The story focuses mostly on the technical approach to modernizing governance. Is there more to it than technology?** Yes. You may recall the classic triad of "People, Process, and Technology," a useful, if simple, way to think about the elements of such a transformation. For the purposes of quick storytelling, we focused on the tech; neglect the people and process aspects at your own risk.

2. **Do I need to be mostly a cloud native organization to pull all this off?** No, but we do see a correlation between maturity in cloud adoption and becoming a high-performing IT organization. Automated governance, like most modern development practices, benefits from the speed and agility offered by cloud computing capabilities.

3. **Does my organization need to have mostly in-house, non third-party developers (like the large tech companies) to pull all this off?** No. Anecdotally, however, there is evidence that such transformations are less challenging when there are less entities to account for, such as various outsourced software development partners who may not embrace the mission as energetically or possess as much agency as in-house developers. There are even examples of hesitance or even authority among third-party development teams to prioritize security fixes with the same enthusiasm as new features. This is likely an understandable, if unfortunate, consequence of contracts signed with third-party development teams being focused on new features being delivered by an agreed upon date; security and compliance efforts like automated governance may thus take a back seat.

4. **If my application portfolio is predominantly made up of certain programming languages or frameworks, will that make any of this easier?** The specific languages or frameworks in use in an organization are less important than the number of languages or frameworks that the organization decides

to officially support. Being intentional about such support and limiting the number of languages or frameworks reduces entropy in the organization and can generally make it easier to get work done together, like automated governance.

5. **Does my organization need to already be a moderate- to high-performing DevOps organization before considering automated governance?** No. There are few truly high-performing DevOps organizations. There are, however, parts of many organizations that are high performing when it comes to DevOps. While maturity in certain aspects of DevOps such as expressing "everything as code" and holistically applying software development best practices across development and operations, DevOps is not strictly a precursor to automated governance. In fact, automated governance can catalyze and accelerate progress along the continuum of the DevOps journey.

6. **Do I need to have already consolidated/homogenized the disparate build pipelines across my organization to pull all this off?** W. Edwards Deming professed that "uncontrolled variation is the enemy of quality". In that spirit, there are clear benefits to standardizing on the infrastructure and workflow that development of software must adhere to. Driving consolidation of the number of build pipelines and their configuration in an organization makes managing software delivery easier because when new practices such as automated governance are to be implemented, there are less environments that may drift and require attention. If your organization has not already taken active steps to do so, consider a formal effort to minimize the "build pipeline sprawl" so automated governance and other optimizations are effective across your software portfolio.

7. **Is a crisis needed for an organization to consider pursuing automated governance?** While crises like receiving an MRIA can focus an organization's attention and will rally action, we do not recommend waiting for a crisis. Instead, we encourage being proactive. You can start small with a few applications in an automated governance effort to demonstrate the value to leadership and earn permission for a broader effort—one that should reduce the likelihood of crises.

ACKNOWLEDGMENTS

When we first assembled to pull together a guidance document about governance, we struggled to get a compelling outline in place. We had several great ideas we wanted to convey, but no matter how we structured it, it was going to be very academic and profoundly dry.

Then we had an idea . . . why not turn it into a short story? That's exactly what we did. Susan, Tim, Bill, Jada, Michelle, Jason, and the rest of the cast sprung to life in a brief narrative to convey what we were trying to capture. The technical guidance paper suddenly became approachable. We were happy with the result, and it seemed the DevOps Enterprise Forum community agreed.

Four months later we got a call . . . "Gene and the staff at IT Revolution have discussed your paper. We want to turn it into a book!" Leah Brown told us. We were stunned and delighted. Leah went on to explain that IT Rev would do some editing and expansion of the narrative so that it would be a short novel. We all agreed that was a great idea. The more we thought about it, the more excited and enthusiastic we all became.

Finally, John Willis said he had another idea. He asked us if we were all willing to invest some additional time and turn this good idea into a great idea and into a full-length novel. We agreed and invited Helen Beal to join our squad of authors.

This book would not have happened without the incredible encouragement of the larger DevOps community. We are indebted to the inspiration and support of the Scenius[1] and the community of leaders from DevOps Enterprise Summit and DevOps Enterprise Forum. Gene and Margueritte Kim are at the top of that list as both the organizers and inspirational leaders of the DevOps movement.

The core concepts presented throughout this book had been brewing through the years in the community, as well as in the form of several DevOps Enterprise Forum guidance papers produced at the annual gathering of community leaders and

---

1 Scenius: Breakthroughs typically emerge from a scene: an exceptionally productive community of practice that develops novel epistemic norms. Brian Eno, who first coined this, wrote, "major innovation may indeed take a genius—but the genius is created in part by a scenius." https://itrevolution. com/love-letter-to-conferences/#why-i-think-virtual-forum-worked-so-well

experts, including many of the authors of this book.[2] Without these papers and their collaborators' vision and research, this book would not exist. We want to mention those foundational papers and their collaborators for their invaluable contribution to the DevOps community:

- *An Unlikely Union: DevOps and Audit* (2015) by James DeLucia, Paul Duvall, Chairman, Mustafa Kapadia, Gene Kim, Dave Mangot, Tapabrata "Topo" Pal, James Wickett, Julie Yoo.
- *Dear Auditor* (2018) by Ben Grinnell, James Wickett, Jennifer Brady, the late Rob Stroud (may he rest in peace), Sam Guckenheimer, Scott Nasello, Tapabrata "Topo" Pal.
- *DevOps Automated Governance* (2019) by Michael Nygard, Tapabrata "Topo" Pal, Stephen Magill, Sam Guckenheimer, John Willis, John Rzeszotarski, Dwayne Holmes, Courtney Kissler, Dan Beauregard, Collette Tauscher.

How do you write a book with nine authors? Cat herding has been an important part of arriving at our destination. We would like to thank Leah Brown for her insightful and supportive sessions with the panel of authors, as well her shepherding of the collaborative editing process. This book would not have happened without her.

Subject matter experts were key to ensure our message stayed relevant and accurate. While this is a work of fiction, our intent was to convey the learning in prose that represented plausible real-world situations. We would like to thank Chris Palumbo for the regulatory insight and Branden Williams and Jen Suiters for their powerful lessons on MRIAs and what regulators would expect.

We would like to thank our peer reviewers, Gene Kim, Courtney Kissler, Emily Fox, Jeff Gallimore, Jennifer Hansen, Cameron Haight, and Maya Senen for their brilliant insight and critical and candid feedback that helped nudge the story from good toward great.

We would also like to thank Brian Scheck, Keith Silvestri, and Mike Onders, whose vision and dedication laid the foundation for many of the stories, learnings, and outcomes in this book.

Even with nine authors, the time investment was significant. We are indebted to our families and loved ones who gave us space to write, encouraged us despite the

---

2 The DevOps Enterprise Forum is an annual event held by IT Revolution, in which industry leaders and experts come together to discuss the most important challenges facing the community. From this event, a series of guidance papers are produced. You can view the full collection of papers here: https://itrevolution.com/resources.

chatty late-night sessions with the group, and the supportive understanding when our noses were buried in our screens typing away at the narrative.

Bill Bensing would like to thank his mom, dad, family, and Kendra for their enduring support. The Nelsons', Tampows', Tingles', and Willis' of the world make these opportunities possible. They, and many others like them, give Bill the friendship, mentoring, and opportunities to be his best. These are the type of people Bill hopes everyone finds in their careers and lives.

Jason Cox would like to thank his wife Jane and their four children, Jonathan, Julia, Jessica, and Jenna. He would also like to thank his incredible team of SREs, fellow technology and business leaders who build magic every day and prove that we can all do the impossible.

Michael Edenzon would like to thank his family: Kathy, Marc, AJ, Zach, Irwin, and Frankie

Tapabrata Pal would like to thank his wife, Chiru, and their two children, Shaily and Ayush.

Caleb Queern would like to thank his wife Marian and his son Joseph.

John Rzeszotarski would like to thank his family: Marla, Sophia, Sebastian, Sawyer, and Simon.

Andres Vega would like to express his deepest gratitude to Olga, Victoria, and Mateo for giving him purpose and constantly challenging him to make Husband and Dad Unlimited thrive. They are the joy and happiness of his life.

And thank you! We are indebted to all of you, the larger community of business and technology leaders who are willing to listen, learn, experiment, and teach. We believe that the future is truly unlimited. With your help, we can all unlock new potential for our businesses, embrace better ways of working, and elevate our human experience across the planet. Thank you for joining us on this journey. Now, let's go change the world!

ABOUT THE AUTHORS

Helen Beal is a DevOps and Ways of Working coach, Chief Ambassador at DevOps Institute, and ambassador for the Continuous Delivery Foundation. She is the Chair of the Value Stream Management Consortium and provides strategic advisory services to DevOps industry leaders. She is also an analyst at Techstrong Research, hosts the Day-to-Day DevOps webinar series for BrightTalk and the Value Stream Evolution series on TechStrong TV. She currently lives in the UK.

Bill Bensing builds things that build things. He is a skilled leader and architect of software, people, teams, and companies. Bill is an expert at making innovation a wholly inclusive process. His love of DevOps comes from a background in logistics and operations management. Automated Governance is a topic Bill finds very interesting. He believes a lack of good governance is the single biggest issue preventing breakthrough value. Bill will tell you, "Good strategy and good governance are the grease and guide rails for success." He lives in the Tampa Bay, FL, area.

Jason Cox is a champion of DevOps practices, promoting new technologies and better ways of working. He enjoys helping organizations deliver more value, better, faster, safer and happier. He is an inspirational speaker who loves people and delights in amplifying their abilities with technology. Jason frequently speaks at conferences, contributes to open source and writes on technical and leadership topics. He currently leads several SRE teams and resides in Los Angeles with his wife and their children.

Michael Edenzon is a senior IT leader and engineer that modernizes and disrupts the technical landscape for highly regulated organizations. Michael provides technical design, decisioning, and solutioning across complex verticals and leverages continuous learning practices to drive organizational change. He is a fervent advocate for the developer experience and believes that enablement-focused automation is the key to building compliant software at scale.

Topo Pal is a thought leader, keynote speaker, evangelist in the areas of DevSec-Ops, Continuous Delivery, Cloud Computing, Open Source Adoption and Digital Transformation. He is a hands-on developer and Open Source contributor. Topo has been leading and contributing to industry initiatives around automated governance in DevOps practices. Topo resides in Richmond, VA, with his wife and two children.

Caleb Queern helps CIOs and CISOs reduce risk across the software development life cycle so they can innovate quickly and win in the market. He lives in Austin, Texas with his wife, Marian, and son, Joseph.

John Rzeszotarski has led organizations with a focus on digital, payments, security, and development. His primary passion is solving complex business and IT problems through technology, fast flow, and building learning organizations. He loves coding new things and driving change in insanely regulated environments. He lives in Pittsburgh, PA, with his family.

Andres Vega helps engineering organizations securely build large-scale, distributed software leveraging novel approaches to reduce the compliance toil associated with the area. He is recognized in the open-source community as a maintainer, contributor, and technical leader focused on the improvement of ecosystem security. Outside of his profession, he is a family guy and an avid outdoors person. You are sure to find him adventuring with his family all over the trails of the San Francisco Bay Area in his best attempt not to get mauled to death by hungry mountain lions.

John Willis is an author and Senior Director of the Global Transformation Office at Red Hat. John is considered one of the founders of the DevOps movement. He lives in Acworth, GA.